WORKBOOK: HOMEWORK AND CHARACTER BOOK
作业和写字簿

to Accompany

Chinese Link
中文天地

Zhōng Wén Tiān Dì

Elementary Chinese

Simplified Character Version

吴素美 Sue-mei Wu
于月明 Yueming Yu
张燕辉 Yanhui Zhang
田维忠 Weizhong Tian

Carnegie Mellon University

PEARSON Prentice Hall
World Languages
Upper Saddle River, New Jersey 07458

Acquisitions Editor: Rachel McCoy
Publishing Coordinator: Claudia Fernandes
Executive Director of Market Development: Kristine Suárez
Director of Editorial Development: Julia Caballero
Production Supervision: Nancy Stevenson
Project Manager: Margaret Chan, Graphicraft
Assistant Director of Production: Mary Rottino
Supplements Editor: Meriel Martínez Moctezuma
Media Editor: Samantha Alducin
Media Production Manager: Roberto Fernandez
Prepress and Manufacturing Buyer: Christina Helder
Prepress and Manufacturing Assistant Manager: Mary Ann Gloriande
Cover Art Director: Jayne Conte
Marketing Assistant: William J. Bliss
Publisher: Phil Miller
Cover image: Jerry Darvin

This book was set in 12/15 Sabon by Graphicraft Ltd., Hong Kong, and was printed and bound by Bradford & Bigelow. The cover was printed by Bradford & Bigelow.

Printed in the United States of America
10 9 8 7 6 5 4 3 2 1

ISBN 0-13-154669-4

Pearson Education Ltd.
Pearson Education Singapore Pte. Ltd.
...son Education Canada, Ltd.
... Education — Japan
...ducation Australia Pty. Limited
...ucation North Asia Ltd.
...ucación de México, S.A. de C.V.
...cation Malaysia Pte. Ltd.

目录 CONTENTS

Character Book Indices

Name: ________________ Date: ____________

拼音作业一 Pinyin Homework I

Simple finals: a o e i u ü *Labial initials: b p m f* *Alveolar initials: d t n l*

1-1 Listen and circle the right final:

1. lǖ	lǘ	lǚ	lǜ	5. dē	dé	dě	dè
2. fū	fú	fǔ	fù	6. mō	mó	mǒ	mò
3. pī	pí	pǐ	pì	7. tī	tí	tǐ	tì
4. nā	ná	nǎ	nà	8. bā	bá	bǎ	bà

1-2 Listen and circle the right initial:

1. mù	nù	4. lǔ	nǔ	7. lǚ	nǚ	10. nǐ	lǐ
2. pā	tā	5. pà	bà	8. bè	tè	11. tā	lā
3. mó	fó	6. tè	lè	9. dí	tí	12. pū	mū

1-3 Listen and fill in the blanks with the right sound:

1. ______	6. ______	11. ______	16. ______
2. ______	7. ______	12. ______	17. ______
3. ______	8. ______	13. ______	18. ______
4. ______	9. ______	14. ______	19. ______
5. ______	10. ______	15. ______	20. ______

拼音作业二 Pinyin Homework II

Velar initials: g k h
Dental sibilant initials: z c s
Palatal initials: j q x
Retroflex initials: zh ch sh r

2-1 Listen and circle the right initial:

1.	qì	xì	6.	zhè	zè	11.	cǐ	sǐ	16.	rè	chè
2.	xī	sī	7.	jī	qī	12.	shú	chú	17.	cā	zā
3.	shī	sī	8.	rì	shì	13.	hù	rù	18.	gé	hé
4.	jǐ	xǐ	9.	zhà	chà	14.	lè	gè	19.	cū	sū
5.	cè	chè	10.	zǔ	sǔ	15.	xì	shì	20.	gē	kē

2-2 Listen and fill in the blank with the right initial:

1. ____ē
2. ____ī
3. ____è
4. ____ī
5. ____ā
6. ____í
7. ____ù
8. ____ì
9. ____ū
10. ____ē
11. ____à
12. ____ú
13. ____ǐ
14. ____è
15. ____ì
16. ____è
17. ____ù
18. ____è
19. ____ǐ
20. ____ì
21. ____é
22. ____á
23. ____ě
24. ____ì
25. ____ū
26. ____ǎ
27. ____ì
28. ____ǔ
29. ____é
30. ____ù

Name: ______________ Date: ______________

拼音作业三 Pinyin Homework III

Compound finals: ai ei ao ou ia iao ie iu ua uo uai ui üe

3-1 Listen and mark the right tones:

1. lao	6. hou	11. kuo	16. nuo
2. cui	7. hua	12. pei	17. hui
3. zhua	8. ai	13. shuo	18. biao
4. liu	9. lüe	14. bie	19. tou
5. ren	10. shuai	15. zhou	20. mao

3-2 Listen and circle the right sounds:

1.	chóu	zhóu	6.	cáo	cái	11.	jiǎo	xiǎo	16.	bǎo	biǎo
2.	chāo	qiāo	7.	lái	léi	12.	bié	béi	17.	shāo	xiāo
3.	dōu	duō	8.	lín	liú	13.	lüè	nüè	18.	luó	lóu
4.	jué	xué	9.	dāo	dōu	14.	xuē	xiū	19.	guò	gòu
5.	huó	hóu	10.	diū	duī	15.	rào	ròu	20.	jiā	jiē

3-3 Listen and fill in the blanks with the right finals:

1. b______	8. l______	15. zh______
2. p______	9. g______	16. ch______
3. m______	10. k______	17. sh______
4. f ______	11. h______	18. r______
5. d______	12. j______	19. z______
6. t______	13. q______	20. c______
7. n______	14. x______	21. s______

拼音作业四 Pinyin Homework IV

Nasal finals: *an en* *ian in* *uan un*
ang eng ong *iang ing iong* *uang*

4-1 Listen and mark the right tones:

1. jiong
2. xian
3. hun
4. an
5. qin
6. lun
7. rong
8. fen
9. cang
10. mian
11. hen
12. qiang
13. heng
14. liang
15. ling
16. nuan
17. zhuang
18. zhun
19. sun
20. ding

4-2 Listen and circle the right sounds:

1. juān jūn
2. zhèn shèn
3. qiáng qióng
4. xiàng xuàn
5. rǎn zhǎn
6. lín líng
7. tūn tuān
8. rēng zhēng
9. kàn kèn
10. qǐng xǐng
11. xióng qióng
12. zhàn zhèn
13. háng huáng
14. huán huáng
15. jūn qūn
16. cóng chóng
17. zhāng jiāng
18. xūn sūn
19. gèn gèng
20. nián lián

4-3 Listen and fill in the blanks with the right finals:

1. b______
2. p______
3. m______
4. f______
5. d______
6. t______
7. n______
8. l______
9. g______
10. k______
11. h______
12. j______
13. q______
14. x______
15. zh______
16. ch______
17. sh______
18. r______
19. z______
20. c______
21. s______

Name: ________________ Date: ____________

拼音作业五 Pinyin Homework V

Special Pinyin and tonal rules

5-1 Listen and fill in the blanks with the right Pinyin:

1. _____	6. _____	11. _____	16. _____
2. _____	7. _____	12. _____	17. _____
3. _____	8. _____	13. _____	18. _____
4. _____	9. _____	14. _____	19. _____
5. _____	10. _____	15. _____	20. _____

5-2 Mark the tones of "yi" (一) and "bu" (不) in accordance with the "yi-bu" tonal rules:

1. ____wǔ____shí 一五一十	6. ____wén____wèn 不闻不问	11. ____ sī____gǒu 一丝不苟
2. ____xīn____yì 一心一意	7. ____míng____bái 不明不白	12. ____ chéng____biàn 一成不变
3. ____zhāo____xī 一朝一夕	8. ____zhé____kòu 不折不扣	13. ____wén____zhí 一文不值
4. ____chàng____hè 一唱一和	9. ____sān____sì 不三不四	14. ____qiào____tōng 一窍不通
5. ____mó____yàng 一模一样	10. ____bēi____kàng 不卑不亢	15. ____chén____rǎn 一尘不染

拼音作业六 Pinyin Homework VI

Comprehensive Pinyin Review

6-1 Listen and circle the right sounds:

1.	dàng	dèng	6.	lǚ	liǔ	11.	yǔ	yǒu	16.	zhàn	jiàn
2.	lǔ	nǚ	7.	bīn	bīng	12.	lián	liáng	17.	yuǎn	yǎn
3.	wō	ōu	8.	niè	lèi	13.	xiōng	jiōng	18.	jiǎo	xiǎo
4.	jié	zéi	9.	dōu	tōu	14.	kǒu	gǒu	19.	xiù	shòu
5.	jūn	zhēn	10.	zuō	cuō	15.	xià	xiào	20.	cāi	sāi

6-2 Listen to the following classroom expressions. Then write them in Pinyin:

1. ______________________________

2. ______________________________

3. ______________________________

4. ______________________________

5. ______________________________

6. ______________________________

7. ______________________________

8. ______________________________

9. ______________________________

10. ______________________________

Name: ________________ Date: ____________

Lesson 1 Hello!

I. Listening Exercises

A. Listen and write out the initials for each of the following words:

1. sh ì (to be / yes) 2. m a 3. x ué sh eng (student)

4. l ǎo sh ī 5. n e 6. b ú

B. Listen and fill in the blanks with appropriate finals:

1. W o sh i x ue sh eng

2. T a b u sh i l ao sh i , t a sh i x ue sh eng.

3. N i y a b u sh i x ue sh eng m a?

C. Listen to the dialogue and then mark each statement below as True (✓) or False (✗):

MARY: 你好！

JOHN: 你好！

MARY: 我是学生，你也是学生吗？

JOHN: 不。我是老师。

 1. Mary 是学生。

 3. Mary 不是学生。

 2. John 也是学生。

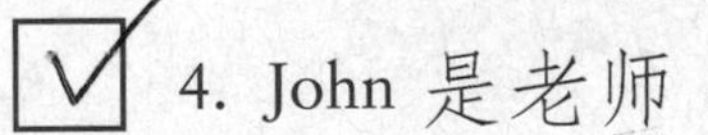 4. John 是老师。

D. Listen to the dialogue again and write it out in Pinyin:

Nǐ hǎo

Nǐ hǎo

wǒ shì xuésheng nǐ yě shì xuésheng ma

bù wǒ shì lǎoshī

II. Character Exercises

A. Write out the characters for the following Pinyin:

1. tā 他　　2. wǒ 我　　3. shì 是　　4. shī 师

5. nǐ 你　　6. xué 学　　7. ne 呢　　8. lǎo 老

9. yě 也　　10. sheng 生　　11. bú 不　　12. hǎo 好

B. Write out the Chinese characters for each of the following words and then show its stroke order:

English	Character	Stroke order
you	wǒ 我	
to be	shì 是	
student	学 xue 生 sheng	

C. Write the Chinese characters for the following English words:

1. he 他　　2. fine 好　　3. teacher 老师

4. I 我　　5. also 也　　6. student 学生

7. not 不　　8. you 你

Name: __________________ Date: _____________

III. Grammar Exercises

A. Fill in the blanks in the following dialogue with "吗" or "呢":

A: 你好!

B: 你好!

A: 我是学生，你也是学生 吗 ?

B: 我也是学生。

A: 他 呢 ? 他也是学生 吗 ?

B: 不，他是老师。

B. Complete the following sentences with the help of the clues:

1. 你 好 。(a greeting)
2. 我 是学生 。(to be a student)
3. 你 也 学生吗? (to be also)
4. 他也 不是 老师。(to be not)
5. 你 呢 ? (question — how about) 你 不是 老师吗? (to be not, either)

C. Insert the words in parentheses at the appropriate place(s) in each sentence. Write the sentences in the space provided.

1. 他学生。(是)
   他是学生 he to be student
2. 我是学生，你是学生? (也、吗)
   我也是学生， 你是学生吗
3. 他是老师，他学生。(不、是)
   ~~他是~~ 他不是老师， 他是学生

IV. Comprehensive Exercises

A. Rearrange the following boxes to form a dialogue. Write the number before each sentence to show the correct order:

Correct order

1. **A:** 你好！

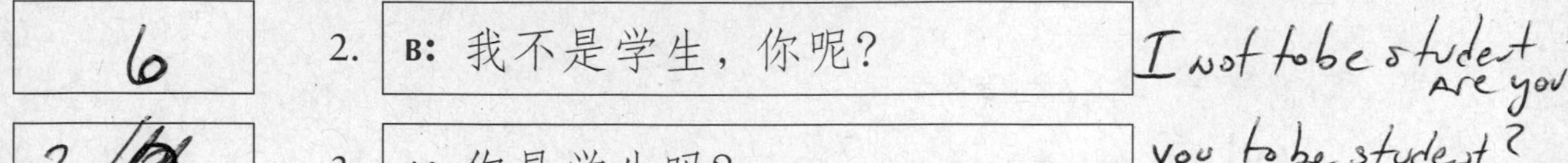

2. **B:** 我不是学生，你呢？

3. **A:** 你是学生吗？
4. **B:** 他也是学生吗？
5. **A:** 不是，他是老师。

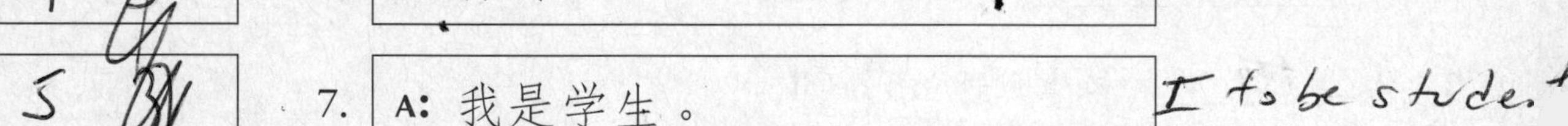

6. **B:** 你好！
7. **A:** 我是学生。

B. Complete the dialogue with the help of the clues:

A: 你好！

B: ______________________________！

A: 我是学生，______________________？

B: 我不是学生，____________________。

A: 他 __________ 老师吗？

B: 是，__________________________。

Name: ________________ Date: ____________

Lesson 2 What's Your Surname?

I. Listening Exercises

A. Listen and circle the correct Pinyin in each pair:

1. qǐngwèn / Yīngwén
2. tóngxué / tóngshì
3. nǐ jiào shénme / nǐ xiào shénme
4. míngcí / míngzi
5. shuí cuò / shéi shuō

B. Listen to the dialogues and circle the correct answer:

1. The person's family name is
   a. Hú.
   b. Lú.
   c. Wú.

2. a. Wenying is a teacher.
   b. Xiaomei's classmate is a teacher.
   c. Dazhong Li is Wenying's classmate.

3. a. Yu Ying's teacher is Xuewen Wu.
   b. Yu Ying is a teacher.
   c. Yu Ying is the man's name.

II. Character Exercises

A. Write out the radicals in the following groups of characters:

 好 她 姓

口 吗 叫 呢

讠 请 谁

B. Write the traditional form of the following characters:

学

谁

师

吗

问

C. Translate the following Pinyin sentences into Chinese:

1. Qǐngwèn, nín shì Lǐ lǎoshī ma?

   请问 您 是 李 老生吗

2. Nǐde tóngxué jiào shénme míngzi?

   你的 同学 叫 什么 名字

III. Grammar Exercises

A. Please use the following clues to make as many sentences as you can. You need to include positive statements, negative statements, and questions. You may use each word as many times as you need:

李， 学文， 叫， 您， 姓， 名字， 中文， 是， 请问， 我

吴， 老师， 她， 于， 的， 小美， 同学， 不， 什么， 吗

Name: ________________ Date: ____________

B. Ask a question on the underlined part in the following sentences (use the underlined part as the answer to your question):

1. 我姓吴。______________________________?
2. 她叫李小英。______________________________?
3. 他是我的同学。______________________________?
4. 我的中文名字是于文汉。______________________________?

C. Translate the following phrases into Chinese:

1. My teacher's name ______________________
2. His classmates ______________________
3. Wenzhong Li's student ______________________
4. Your Chinese name ______________________
5. Her student's Chinese name ______________________

IV. Comprehensive Exercises

A. Complete the following dialogue:

A: 你好！请问，____________?

B: 我______李，______学文。你呢?

A: ______叫吴小英。我______学生。

B: 她是______? 她__________学生吗?

A: 不，她是______。

B: 她是______中文老师吗?

A: 不，______我的英文老师。

B. You introduced yourself to all the students in the Chinese class today. Write down what you said in class about yourself. You may add whatever information you want to help others know you better (approximately 50 characters).

Name: ____________ Date: ____________

Lesson 3 Which Country Are You From?

I. Listening Exercises

A. Listen and circle the six words you hear:

1. Fǎguó
2. shòumìng
3. Zhōngwén
4. Měilìjiān
5. bāgè
6. Shuōmíng
7. měiyìjiā
8. chōngwén
9. Yīngwén
10. nǎr

B. Listen and add the correct tone mark(s) to the following Pinyin:

1. cong
2. Hanyu
3. xuexi
4. nar
5. mingtian
6. guojia
7. yuyan
8. xingming
9. jiaoshou
10. shuohua

C. Listen to the dialogue and write it out in Pinyin, paying special attention to the tones:

____

____

____

____

II. Character Exercises

A. Write out each stroke of the following characters in the appropriate order:

国 ____

美 ____

说 ____

哪 ____

B. Write out as many characters as you can that use the radicals below:

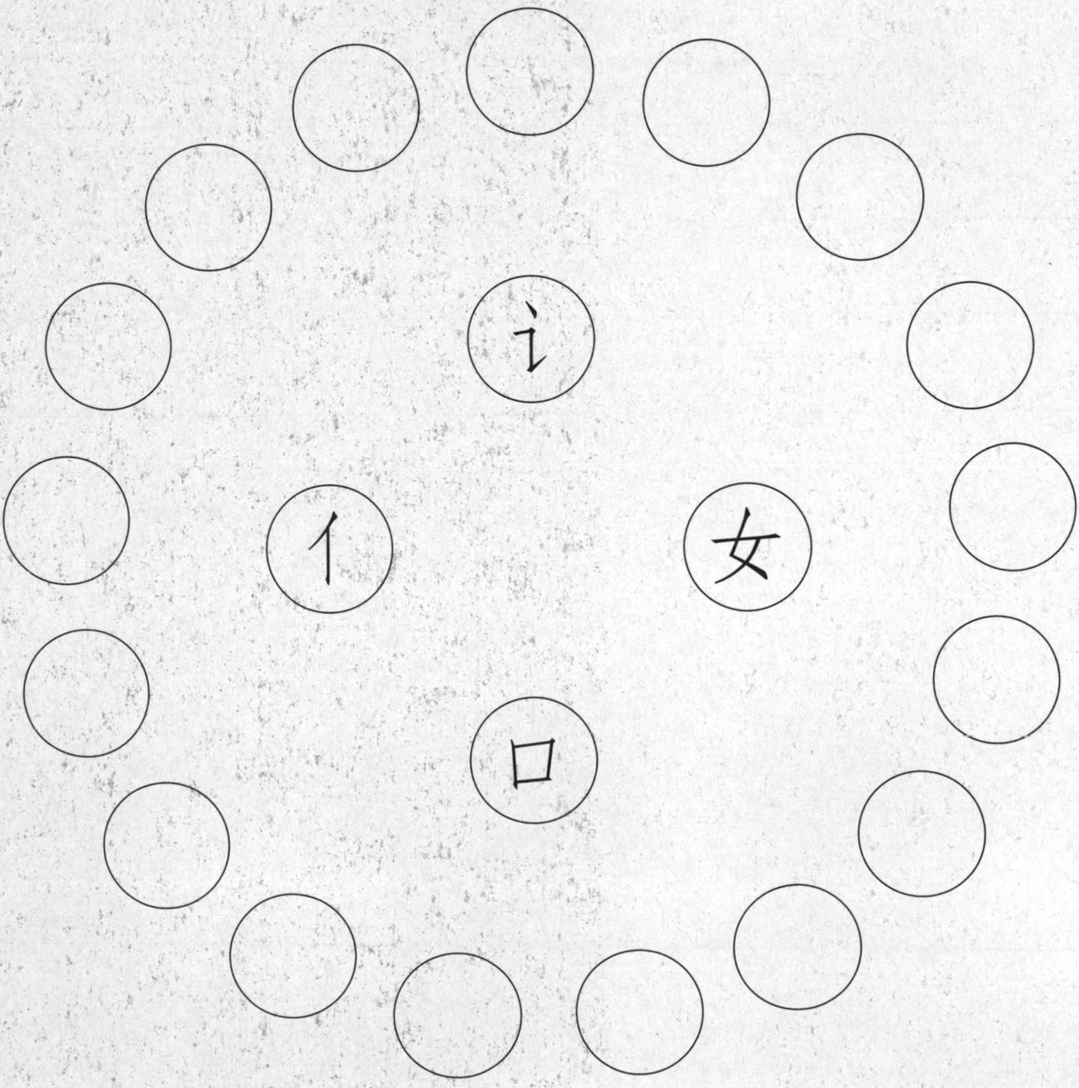

Name: ________________ Date: ____________

III. Grammar Exercises

A. Complete the following sentences with the help of the clues:

1. 你是 __________ 人?

   我是 ________________ 。 (英国)

2. 我是 ________________人。 (中国)

   我说 __________________ 。

3. 他是 ________________ 。

   他教 ________________ 。 (英文)

Note: 教 [jiāo]: to teach

4. 我会 _________________ 。 (英)

   我也会 ________________ 。 (法)

B. Complete the following sentences:

1. 小文是 ___________，他 ______ 中文。
2. 李小美 _____ 法国人，她 ____ 说英文，她说 ______ 。
3. 她 ____ 美国人，她说 ________，她 ____ 说 ________ 日文。

Note: 日文 [Rìwén]: Japanese language

IV. Comprehensive Exercises

Someone asks you about your friend who is also in your class. Use the list you compiled in class as a reference to introduce him/her to others. Write as much as you can about your friend (approximately 60 characters).

Name: ____________________ Date: ______________

Lesson 4 What Do You Study?

I. Listening Exercises

A. Listen to the dialogues and fill in the blanks with Pinyin:

1. Zhè shì shénme?

   Zhè shì ________________________________.

   Gōngchéng ______________?

   ______________.

2. ____________ shéi?

   Nà shì ____________________________.

   Tā ________ ma?

   Tā __________________.

3. Nǐ xué ______________?

   Wǒ xué _____________.

   Zhōngwén ______________?

   Bú _____________, kěshì ____________________.

II. Character Exercises

A. Write out the Chinese character for each of the following words and then show its stroke order:

English	Character	Stroke order
this		
difficult		
engineering		
homework		

B. Give the radical for the following characters and see whether you can provide more examples of characters with the same radical:

	Radical	Examples
1. 课		______________
2. 你		______________
3. 吗		______________

Name: ____________ Date: ____________

III. Grammar Exercises

A. Ask as many questions as you can on the following sentences:

Example:	这是中文书。 —这是什么? —这是什么书?

1. 这是文中的一本工程书。

___

___

___

2. 工程课的功课很多。

___

___

___

3. 英国文学不太难。

___

___

___

4. 中文功课很多，也很难。

___

___

___

IV. Comprehensive Exercises

A. Translate the following sentences into Chinese:

1. Who is he? He is my Chinese literature professor.

   ____

2. What is that? That is an engineering book. That is a book in English.

   ____

3. What do you study? I study French literature. French literature is not very difficult, but there is a lot of homework.

   ____

B. You are going to attend a meeting called by your department. The meeting is to collect your comments on your study and life on campus. The department needs to have some basic information about you before the meeting. Write out a paragraph to introduce yourself (approximately 70 characters).

____

____

____

____

____

____

____

____

Name: ____________ Date: ____________

Lesson 5 This Is My Friend

I. Listening Exercises

A. Listen to the dialogue and mark each of the following sentences with a "✓" if it is correct, an "✗" if it is wrong:

☐ 1. Xiǎohóng de shìyǒu jiào Měiwén.

☐ 2. Měiwén hé Fāng Míng dōu shì Zhōngguórén.

☐ 3. Fāng Míng jièshào tāde péngyou Xiǎohóng.

☐ 4. Měiwén cháng gēn Xiǎohóng shuō Zhōngwén.

☐ 5. Xiǎohóng yǒu liǎngge Měiguó shìyǒu.

B. Listen to the dialogue and fill in the blanks with correct words or expressions:

吴小英：大文，我来 ________ 一下。________ 我室友王小红。

李大文：________ 李大文。你好！

王小红：你好！你是学生 ______？

李大文：是。我 ______ 工程。你 ______？

王小红：我学 ________。我 _____ 小英 _____ 同学。我们 ____ 学 ________ 文学。

II. Character Exercises

A. Pick from this lesson as many characters as you can that start with a horizontal stroke (一):

1. ______ 2. ______ 3. ______ 4. ______ 5. ______ 6. ______

7. ______

With a vertical stroke (丨):

1. ______ 2. ______

With a left-slanted stroke (丿):

1. ______ 2. ______ 3. ______ 4. ______ 5. ______ 6. ______

7. ______

B. Turn the following Pinyin into characters:

1. liǎngge péngyou ____

2. jǐge shìyǒu ____

3. jièshào yíxià ____

4. cháng shuō Zhōngwén ____

Name: ______________ Date: ______________

III. Grammar Exercises

A. Fill in the blanks in the following paragraph. Read it carefully and then ask as many questions on the paragraph as you can:

方美文 ______ 中文班的学生。她 ______ 一个室友，______ 王文英。

王文英 ______ 中国人。她 ______ 一个男朋友，______ 李中。

李中是美国 ______，他 ______ 学中文。他常 ______ 文英说中文。

他们 ______ 是好朋友。

Note: 班 [bān]: class

____

____

____

____

____

____

____

____

IV. Comprehensive Exercises

You share an apartment with your classmates, Wáng Fāng and Lǐ Yīng. You have invited your friend Wú Xiǎowén to come for a party at your apartment. Introduce them and then have a conversation. Write out the conversation using as much from the lesson as you can.

Name: ____________________ Date: ______________

Lesson 6 My Family

I. Listening Exercises

A. Listen, then read the following sentences. Mark "✓" if the statement is correct, and "✗" if it is wrong:

☐ 1. Jiāmíng hé Yǒupéng dōushì cóng Táiwān lái de.

☐ 2. Yǒupéng de bàba bù hěn máng.

☐ 3. Jiāmíng méiyǒu nán péngyou, tā jiějie yǒu.

☐ 4. Yǒupéng de jiā búzài Niǔyuē, zài Bōshìdùn.

☐ 5. Jiāmíng de mèimei méiyǒu māo, yǒu liǎngzhī gǒu.

B. Listen to the paragraph and answer the questions in Pinyin:

1. ______________________________

2. ______________________________

3. ______________________________

4. ______________________________

5. ______________________________

II. Character Exercises

A. Circle the radicals in the following characters:

1. 辆 2. 爸 3. 姐 4. 程

5. 作 6. 狗 7. 没 8. 课

B. Write the following sentences in characters:

1. Wǒ jiā yǒu sìge rén. ______________________

2. Jiějie yǒu yíge nán péngyou. ______________________

3. Bàba, māma dōu shì zài Měiguó gōngzuò de. ______________________

4. Wǒ yǒu liǎngzhī gǒu. ______________________

5. Wǒ hěn ài wǒde jiā. ______________________

III. Grammar Exercises

A. Fill in the blank of each phrase with a proper measure word (classifier):

1. 一 _____ 车　　2. 一 _____ 狗

3. 两 _____ 学生　　4. 三 ______ 书

B. Fill in the blanks in the following paragraph and then ask questions on the highlighted parts:

小美的家__________。他家有________人：爸爸、妈妈、姐姐和她。爸爸、妈妈都在纽约________。爸爸有两______车，______是日本车。姐姐_____有一辆车，是德国车。姐姐的男朋友_____家文，他是__________来的。

Note: 波士顿 [Bōshìdùn]: Boston

____

____

____

____

____

____

Name: ______________ Date: ______________

IV. Comprehensive Exercises

A. Translate the following sentences into Chinese:

1. Both Xiaoying and her boyfriend are from China.

____

2. My roommate has an American car.

____

3. There are four people in my family. We all love our family.

____

B. You received an email from 李书文, a student in China who is looking for a pen pal. You have been looking for a Chinese pen pal for a while. Now you want to take this opportunity to make friends with him. Write an introduction about yourself and then ask him some questions to get to know him better.

Note: 笔友 [bǐyǒu]: pen pal

____

____

____

____

____

Name: ____________ Date: ____________

Lesson 7 Where Do You Live?

I. Listening Exercises

A. Listen to the dialogue and circle the right answer:

1. 小美住在哪儿?
   a. 住在宿舍。
   b. 住在校外。
   c. 住在朋友家。
   d. 住在公寓。

2. 小美的房间号码是多少?
   a 二三五
   b. 五二三
   c. 九二三
   d. 二八五

3. 小美的手机号码是多少?
   a. 三三二 二六八七四六九
   b. 七七二 二二八四七六九
   c. 五三三 六八六二四九七
   d. 八八二 九二八四六七三

4. 小美有几个室友?
   a. 二个
   b. 两个
   c. 三个
   d. 一个

B. Listen to the dialogue and fill in the blanks with the correct Pinyin:

常小西：书文，你住在那个 ____ 吗?

程书文：不，我住在 ____，房间号码是 ____。

常小西：你的 ____ 有 ____ 吗?

程书文：没有 ____，可是我有 ____。

常小西：号码是 ____?

程书文：号码是 ____。

Note: 公寓 [gōngyù]: apartment

II. Character Exercises

A. Comprehensive character exercises:

Process 1: Write down the radical.

Process 2: Count strokes of the character.

Process 3: Write down the correct Pinyin for the character.

Process 4: Make as many words or phrases using the character as you can.

Example: 房 → 户 → 8 → fáng → 房间

	Radical	No. of strokes	Pinyin	Word
1. 间				
2. 号				
3. 校				
4. 机				

B. Write down the traditional form of the framed characters.

1. 哪 儿 ________
2. 号 码 ________
3. 房 间 ________
4. 电 话 ________
5. 手 机 ________

Name: ____________________ Date: ____________

III. Grammar Exercises

A. 大王 and 小李 are in the same Chinese class. They often work together in class. Now the professor asks them to find out each other's contact information for future use. Complete the conversation by filling in the blanks with what you have learned in this lesson:

大王：小李，你 ____ 在宿舍吗？

小李：对了，我 ____ 在学校的 _______。你 ____ 住在学校的宿舍吗？

大王：不，我住在校外，在 ____________________________
(Number 89764 Fifth Ave.)

小李：你的房间 _______ 吗？

大王：很大，_____ 很好。你住在 ___________？

小李：二〇八号。我的房间 _____ 不小。你的电话号码 _________？

大王：___________________________ (103-952-8467)

小李：我的电话号码 _______ 六四八二五三一。

Note: 对了 [duìle]: yes, correct; by the way

Hint: Fifth Ave.: 第五大街 [dì wǔ dàjiē]

B. Translate the following sentences into Chinese:

1. Where do you live?

____

2. Do you live on campus?

____

3. My brother's dorm is not big.

____

4. Your cellular phone number is (142)268-5738, isn't it?

____

IV. Comprehensive Exercises

Write a note:

Your close friend is going to visit you over the weekend. Please write a short note providing necessary information such as your address, phone number, and roommates' names, etc.

Name: ________________ Date: ____________

Lesson 8 Do You Know Him?

I. Listening Exercises

A. Listen to the sentences. Translate the question into English and write the answer in Pinyin:

> Example:
>
> Dialogue on the tape:
>
> 韩文英：你认识的中国同学多不多？
> 谢国友：很多。
>
> *Your answers:*
>
> Translated question: *Do you know a lot of Chinese students?*
> Pinyin answer: *Hěnduō.*

1. Translated question: Is that your Chinese book? Na shi ni de zhongwen shu dui me

   Pinyin answer: dui, na shi wo de zhongwen shu

2. Translated question: Are you from France Ni shi cong faguo lai de shi bu shi

   Pinyin answer: wo sh cong faguo laide

3. Translated question: Are you busy today ni jintian mang bu mang

   Pinyin answer: wo jintian bu ma

4. Translated question: Do you have a lot of homework Nide gongke duo bu duo

   Pinyin answer: hen duo

5. Translated question: Is your friends home big? Ni pengyou dajia da bu da

   Pinyin answer: Ta dajia bu da

B. Listen to the dialogue and circle the correct answer:

1. 德朋是从哪儿来的?

a. 中国　　b. 韩国　　c. 纽约　　d. 日本

2. 文中、德朋和王红今天想去吃什么菜?

a. 中国菜　　b. 韩国菜　　c. 泰国菜　　d. 日本菜

3. 他们下次想去吃什么菜?

a. 中国菜　　b. 韩国菜　　c. 泰国菜　　d. 日本菜

II. Character Exercises

A. Write down the traditional forms of the following characters, and then mark their radicals:

Example: 么 麼 丿

	Traditional form	Radical		Traditional form	Radical		Traditional form	Radical
1. 认			2. 识			3. 课		
4. 后			5. 饭			6. 样		

B. Write the following sentences in characters:

1. Nǐ yǒu shénme shèr ma?

____

2. Nǐ xiǎng bù xiǎng huí jiā?

____

3. Wǒmen yìqǐ qù Zhōngguó, hǎo bù hǎo?

____

4. Xiàkè yǐhòu wǒ xiǎng qù péngyou jiā.

____

5. Wǒ bú rènshi nà ge gōngchéngshī.

____

Name: ____________________ Date: ______________

III. Grammar Exercises

A. Change the following sentences into interrogative forms by adding the words given in the brackets at the appropriate places:

1. 吴小美是学工程的。 (是吗)

____

2. 她今天想回家。 (A 不 A)

____

3. 张友朋认识我姐姐。 (对不对)

____

4. 他的两个室友都是美国人。 (吗)

____

5. 我们下次一起去纽约。 (怎么样)

____

6. 下课以后我去吃饭。 (A 不 A)

____

B. Translate the following sentences into Chinese:

1. Where are you going?

____

2. I have a plan for after class.

____

3. Do you want to have dinner with us tonight?

____

4. My friend doesn't know our English teacher.

____

IV. Comprehensive Exercises

Write a dialogue:

You are going to invite your Chinese friend, 文英, to watch an American movie after class. Please write down the short dialogue between you and 文英. Please use more "A 不 A" questions and tag questions in the dialogue.

Name: ____________ Date: ____________

Lesson 9 He Is Making a Phone Call

I. Listening Exercises

A. Listen to the dialogue and circle the right answer:

1. 丁明在哪儿?
   a. 在纽约
   b. 在他的房间
   c. 在朋友家
   d. 在宿舍

2. 丁明在做什么?
   a. 在看电视
   b. 在练习中文
   c. 在上课
   d. 在吃日本菜

3. 今天晚上丁明想做什么?
   a. 想看电影
   b. 想去朋友家
   c. 想看小说
   d. 想上网

4. 和丁明打电话的是谁?
   a. 爱文
   b. 小美
   c. 丁明的妹妹
   d. 王红

B. Listen to the telephone messages and mark the correct statements with "✓" and the incorrect ones with "✗":

☐ 1. 电话是小西的同学打来的。

☐ 2. 打电话的人今天晚上想和小西一起去看电影。

☐ 3. 他的电话号码是(一四二)三六六七八九二。

Note: 电影 [diànyǐng]: movie

II. Pinyin and Character Exercises

A. Circle the correct Pinyin to match the words:

1. 正在	zèngzài	zhèngzài	zèngzhài
2. 房间	hángjiān	féngjiàn	fángjiān
3. 电视	diànsì	diànshì	diánshì
4. 上网	shángwǎng	shàngwǎng	shánghuǎng
5. 时候	shíhou	shéhou	chíhou
6. 今天	zīntiān	jíntian	jīntiān
7. 晚上	wǎngsàng	wánchàng	wǎnshàng
8. 留言	lúyán	niúyán	liúyán
9. 再见	zàijiàn	zhàijiàn	zhuáizhuàn
10. 知道	jīdào	jīdòu	zhīdào

B. Comprehensive character exercises:

Process 1: Write down the radical.

Process 2: Count strokes of the character.

Process 3: Write down the correct Pinyin for the character.

Process 4: Make as many words or phrases using the character as you can.

Example: 话 → 讠 → 8 → huà → 电话

	Radical	No. of strokes	Pinyin	Word
1. 今				
2. 看				
3. 电				
4. 忙				

Name: ________________ Date: ____________

C. Write down the traditional form of the framed characters:

1. 打 [电][话] ________
2. 看 [电][视] ________
3. 上 [网] ________
4. 看 [书] ________
5. [对] 不 起 ________
6. [时] 候 ________
7. [谢谢] ________
8. [给] ________

III. Grammar Exercises

A. Complete the sentences with "正在……" and the phrases given:

1. **A:** 请问小文在吗？

   B: 在，他 ____________________。(看电视)

2. **A:** 丁老师呢？

   B: 她 ____________________。(休息)

3. **A:** 姐姐呢？

   B: 她 ____________________。(和男朋友打电话)

4. **A:** 王红和小美都在学中文吗？

   B: 王红没有在学中文。她 ____________________。(学法文)

B. Translate the following sentences into Chinese:

1. Do you want to leave a message?

2. Please ask him to call me when he is back.

3. May I ask who is speaking, please?

4. He is not watching TV. He is on the Internet.

5. Hold on, please.

IV. Comprehensive Exercises

Leave a message:

You want to go to 小文's dorm to ask him some questions on mathematics this evening, but 小文 is not available when you visit him. Compose a message to leave on his answering machine, telling him about your plan and asking him to call you back when he returns.

Name: ____________ Date: ____________

Lesson 10 I Get Up at 7:30 Every Day

I. Listening Exercises

A. Listen to 小美's daily schedule of her summer Chinese course in Shanghai, and then mark the correct statements with "✓" and the incorrect ones with "✗":

☐ 1. 小美每天早上八点起床。

☐ 2. 然后九点去学校上课。

☐ 3. 下课以后，小美去图书馆看书。

☐ 4. 下午小美上中文课。

☐ 5. 中文课以后，小美去打球。

B. Listen to 友朋 talk about his daily schedule and write out the time of each activity in Chinese:

1. 起床 ________	2. 睡觉 ________	3. 上课 ________	4. 吃晚饭 ________
5. 去图书馆 ________	6. 打球 ________	7. 学中文 ________	8. 上网 ________

II. Pinyin and Character Exercises

Write out the Pinyin and characters for the following English words or phrases:

	Pinyin	*character*		*Pinyin*	*character*
1. university	________	________	2. semester	________	________
3. everyday	________	________	4. life	________	________
5. email	________	________	6. library	________	________
7. then	________	________	8. like	________	________
9. write letter	________	________	10. play ball	________	________
11. get up	________	________	12. go to bed	________	________

III. Grammar Exercises

A. The following time and activities show what 文英 does every day. Write a paragraph about her daily activities:

10:30 A.M. (use "才")	get up
11:30 A.M. every day	take courses
after class	play ball
4:00 P.M.	study in the library
8:30 P.M.	write emails
12:15 A.M.	sleep

____

____

____

____

____

____

B. Translate the following sentences into Chinese:

1. He went to have Japanese food at 12:30. After that, he went to the library.

   ____

2. I wrote a letter to my elder sister after getting up.

   ____

3. He plays ball at 9:00 P.M. every day.

   ____

4. I like my university life.

   ____

Name: ____________ Date: ____________

IV. Comprehensive Exercises

Short essay:

Write a letter describing your university life to your parents.

Lesson 11 Do You Want Black Tea or Green Tea?

I. Listening Exercises

A. Listen to the dialogue and mark the correct statements with "✓" and the incorrect ones with "✗":

☐ 1. 小美和于英正在法国饭馆吃饭。

☐ 2. 小美正在喝汤。

☐ 3. 饭馆的牛肉很好吃。

☐ 4. 于英不喜欢喝可乐。

B. Listen to the telephone conversation between 方小文 and a waitress in a Chinese restaurant. Check the items and circle the numbers 方小文 has ordered for pick-up.

Note: 拿 [ná]: pick up

方小文点的菜：

☐	啤酒	1	2	3	4	5	
☐	可乐	1	2	3	4	5	  
☐	冰红茶	1	2	3	4	5	 
☐	汤	1	2	3	4	5	 
☐	炒饭	1	2	3	4	5	 
☐	炒面	1	2	3	4	5	 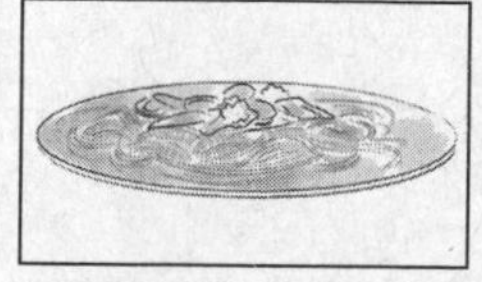
☐	饺子	10	20	30	40	50	

II. Character Exercises

A. Write the characters for the following words:

1. xǐhuān		2. háishì	
3. píjiǔ		4. lǜchá	
5. chǎomiàn		6. kělè	
7. chǎofàn		8. xiǎng	
9. fànguǎn		10. bīnghóngchá	
11. xiānsheng		12. xiǎojiě	
13. fúwùyuán		14. jiǎozi	
15. shuāng		16. pán	

Name: ________________ Date: ____________

B. Write out the radicals for the following characters, count their stroke numbers, and look up their meanings in the dictionary and enter on chart:

Characters	Radical	No. of strokes	Definition
馆	饣	11	house
务			
坐			
员			
喝			
茶			
杯			
红			
冰			
乐			
瓶			
酒			
盘			
面			
筷			

III. Grammar Exercises

A. Ask an alternative question based on the choices given and then answer it:

1. 吃中国菜，吃法国菜

   ______________________________?

   ____

2. 去打球，去图书馆

   ______________________________?

   ____

3. 两点下课，三点下课

   ______________________________?

   ____

4. 是工程师，是老师

   ______________________________?

   ____

5. 有四门课，有五门课

   ______________________________?

   ____

Name: ________________ Date: ____________

B. Fill in the blanks with the proper measure words (some of them may be used more than once):

位　只　个　杯　瓶　辆　盘　碗　双　本

1. 常先生是一___很好的老师。
2. 我点两___炒饭和两___可乐。
3. 爸爸有一___狗。
4. 我们家有四___人。
5. 她想喝一___茶。
6. 我的朋友要一___啤酒。
7. 那个美国人有一___车。
8. 那三___法国人想喝一___冰红茶和两___咖啡。
9. 这五___学生有三___工程书。
10. 给我们三___汤和一___筷子。

C. Translate the following sentences into Chinese:

1. Do you like drinking tea or coffee?

____

2. Which subject do you like to study, literature or engineering?

____

3. After eating the fried rice, I want to drink a cup of tea.

____

4. I often go to Chinese restaurants.

____

IV. Comprehensive Exercises

Three old friends of yours are coming to your apartment for a visit in the evening. But you are unfortunately unable to prepare food for them. You leave a note to your roommate and ask him/her to do you a favor by ordering food from the Chinese restaurant (at least 70 characters). Please include the following words and phrases in the note:

点　要　想　喜欢　杯　瓶　盘　碗　双　谢谢

Name: ________________ Date: ____________

Lesson 12 May I Borrow Your Car?

I. Listening Exercises

A. Listen to the following sentences, fill in the blanks, and then translate the sentences into English:

1. 他 ___ 知道我 ___ 不 ___ 在他的家吃晚饭。

   ____

2. 你 ___ ___ 少喝一点儿咖啡。

   ____

3. 小李 ___ 开车去学校的图书馆 ___ 两本 ___ ___ ___ ___ 书。

   ____

4. ___ 纽约开车 ___ 洛杉矶 ___ ___ 五天。

   ____

5. 今年五月我 ___ 回家看妈妈。

   ____

6. 我明天 ___ ___ 用我朋友 ___ ___ 我的电脑 ___ 小王写电子邮件。

   ____

Notes: 纽约 [Niǔyuē]: New York
洛杉矶 [Luòshānjī]: Los Angeles
电脑 [diànnǎo]: computer

B. Listen to the dialogue between 方明英 and 丁文, and then mark the correct statements with "✓" and the incorrect ones with "✗":

☐ 1. 丁明很想看这个中国电影。
☐ 2. 丁文明天下午没有课。
☐ 3. 每天下午有车从宿舍到中美图书馆。
☐ 4. 丁文要跟方明英一起看电影。

Note: 电影 [diànyǐng]: movie

II. Character Exercises

A. Comprehensive character exercises:

Process 1: Write down the radical.

Process 2: Count strokes of the character.

Process 3: Write down the correct Pinyin for the character.

Process 4: Make as many words or phrases with the character as you can.

Example: 机 → 木 → 6 → jī → 计算机、手机、飞机、机场

	Radical	No. of strokes	Pinyin	Word
1. 场				
2. 习				
3. 进				
4. 样				

B. Circle all the simplified characters in the following dialogue and then provide their traditional forms:

王家欢：于飞，你的电脑可以看中文，是吗？

于　飞：对，有什么事儿吗？

王家欢：我要上网找中文资料，可以借你的电脑用一下儿吗？

于　飞：没问题。现在我不用电脑，可是吃饭以后我要用电脑做作业。

王家欢：知道了，谢谢！

于　飞：不客气。

Notes: 找 [zhǎo]: look for
资料 [zīliào]: material

1. ______ 2. ______ 3. ______ 4. ______ 5. ______

6. ______ 7. ______ 8. ______ 9. ______ 10. ______

11. ______ 12. ______ 13. ______ 14. ______ 15. ______

Name: ________________ Date: ____________

III. Grammar Exercises

A. Fill in the blanks with the following optative words:

要，想，应该，得，能，可以，会

1. 他们 _____ 坐飞机从纽约来这儿玩儿。
2. 我的爸爸妈妈都 _____ 说中文，你 _____ _____ 跟他们说中文。
3. 她 _____ _____ 会开手排挡的车。
4. 我今天晚上 _____ 借你的车吗？

B. Write the negations of the following sentences:

1. 我要在早上六点起床。

____

2. 我们想多喝点茶。

____

3. 小美应该多练习开车。

____

4. 我能借老师的书。

____

5. 在宿舍可以看电视。

____

6. 老师今天会晚点儿下课。

____

7. 你得开车去机场。

____

C. Translate the following sentences into Chinese:

1. I want to borrow a Chinese novel from the library, but I don't know which one is good.

   ____

2. Can you give a brief introduction about Shanghai?

   ____

3. I can speak Chinese, know a lot of characters, and can write a little Chinese.

   ____

4. What will you do after you are back in your dormitory?

   ____

IV. Comprehensive Exercises

Read the following passage and answer the questions which follow:

我叫李红英，我在华中大学学工程。我的爸爸妈妈都是中国人，可是我在美国出生，也在美国长大 [zhǎngdà] (grow up)。我小的时候，爸爸妈妈说我应该学中文。可是我不喜欢学中文。爸爸妈妈跟我说中文的时候，我总是 [zǒngshì] (always) 跟他们说英文。

上大学以后我认识到 [rènshidào] (realize) 学中文很重要，于是 [yúshì] (therefore) 我非常想学中文了。去年八月的时候，我去问 [wèn] (ask) 华中大学中文系的王老师我应该上哪个中文班。王老师问我的中文怎么样。我说我能说一点儿中文，可是我一个中文字也不会写。王老师说我应该在一年级 [yī niánjí] (Grade One) 学中文。

我从去年九月到十二月在华中大学学中文。现在我已经 [yǐjīng] (already) 能说很多句子，还能读，也能写二百五十个中文字了。

这个学期我要继续学中文。今年夏天 [xiàtiān] (summer) 我想去中国学习，这样就能多跟中国人说中文，我的中文也一定 [yídìng] (must) 能进步。

Name: ________________ Date: ____________

1. 李红英在哪个大学学习？她的专业 [zhuānyè] (major) 是什么？

____

2. 李红英小的时候跟爸爸妈妈说中文吗？

____

3. 上中文课以前，李红英会说中文、写中文吗？

____

4. 王老师说李红英应该上哪个中文班？

____

5. 李红英是从去年几月到几月在大学学习中文的？

____

6. 今年夏天李红英要做什么？

____

Name: ______________ Date: ____________

Lesson 13 I Want to Buy a Shirt

I. Listening Exercises

A. Listen to the dialogue and read the following statements. Mark the correct statements with "✓" and the incorrect ones with "✗".

☐ 1. 方明飞想买一件衬衫。

☐ 2. 店员要他试试蓝色的牛仔裤。

☐ 3. 方明飞喜欢黑色的牛仔裤。

☐ 4. 店员说黄衬衫很好看。

☐ 5. 方明飞说黑色的衬衫很不错。

B. Listen to the statements and fill in the blanks with appropriate words:

1. 我想买一 ____ 衬衫 ________ 一条裤子。

2. 你 ________ 看看。我 ______ 这件好吗?

3. 这条裙子 ____________?

4. 请 ___________ 。

5. 我 ________ 喜欢黑色的。

II. Character Exercises

A. Circle all the simplified characters in the following dialogue and then provide their traditional forms:

钱　飞：小天，你帮我看看，我穿这件衬衫怎么样？

张小天：我觉得那件黄的好看。这件黑的不太好看。

钱　飞：好，我试试那件黄的。不错，我很喜欢。你呢？你想买什么？

张小天：我想买一条裙子或者一条裤子。

钱　飞：裙子和裤子都买吧。

张小天：好，我都买。

1. ______ 2. ______ 3. ______ 4. ______ 5. ______

6. ______ 7. ______ 8. ______ 9. ______ 10. ______

11. ______ 12. ______ 13. ______ 14. ______ 15. ______

B. Write the characters for the following Pinyin words and group them according to their radicals in the chart provided:

1. wèi ______ 2. chuān ______ 3. tiáo ______ 4. mǎi ______

5. qún ______ 6. ràng ______ 7. shì ______ 8. shān ______

9. chèn ______ 10. jiā ______ 11. jiàn ______ 12. yuán ______

Group no.	Radical	Characters with the radical
1		
2		
3		
4		
5		
6		
7		
8		

Name: ______________ Date: ____________

III. Grammar Exercises

A. Fill in each blank with an appropriate measure word:

1. 一 __________ 裤子
2. 两 __________ 衬衫
3. 三 __________ 鞋
4. 四 __________ 裙子
5. 五 __________ 牛仔裤
6. 六 __________ 运动衫
7. 七 __________ 小狗
8. 八 __________ 电影票

B. Complete the following dialogues based on the clues given:

1. 你说那件衬衫怎么样?

   ______________________________。
   (Let me have a look.)

2. 我应该穿几号的?

   ____。
   (Try size 6 or size 7.)

3. 我不知道这个电影是说什么的。

   _________________________。
   (I'll give you a little introduction.)

4. 上海春卷真好吃。

   真的吗? ______________________________________。
   (I'll taste it as well.)

5. 手排挡的车我还不会开。

   _________________________。
   (You should learn it.)

C. Answer the following questions using the expression "或者":

1. 你想买什么?

2. 这张电影票是谁的?

3. 我们去哪个餐馆吃饭?

4. 你喜欢黄衬衫吗?

IV. Comprehensive Exercises

Describe a recent shopping trip (about 80–100 characters).

Name: ____________ Date: ____________

Lesson 14 I Am 20 This Year

I. Listening Exercises

A. Listen to the sentences and fill in the blanks with the missing characters:

1. 三月十八日是我的 ________ 。
2. 我今年 ________ , ________ 二十岁 。
3. ________ 是我的生日 ________ 。请你 ________ 。

B. Listen to the dialogue, then mark the correct statements with "✓" and the incorrect ones with "✗":

☐ 1. 星星今年二十岁 。
☐ 2. 明明下个星期五要过生日 。
☐ 3. 星星下个星期五晚上没有空 。
☐ 4. 方明明的妈妈要做一个蛋糕 。
☐ 5. 方明明要吃两块蛋糕 。

II. Character Exercises

A. Following are the characters from the lesson. For each one:

1. Identify the radical.
2. Count the number of strokes.
3. Give the English definition.
4. Provide more characters with the same radical.

Character	Radical	No. of strokes	English	More examples
家				
送				
地				
星				
棒				

B. Write the following Pinyin sentences in Chinese characters:

1. Wǒde shēngrì shì yīyuè sān shí hào, xīngqīsì.

____

2. Zhè shì nǐde péngyou sòng nǐde dà dàngāo ma?

____

3. Nǐ jīnnián duō dà? Wǒ jīnnián shíjiǔ suì.

____

III. Grammar Exercises

A. Find the following dates from this year's calendar and fill in the blanks:

1. 今年春节 [Chūnjié] (Spring Festival / Chinese New Year) 是 __________ (date), __________ (weekday) 。
2. 今天是 __________ (date), __________ (weekday) 。
3. 下个星期日是 __________ (date) 。
4. 今年的感恩节 [Gǎn'ēnjié] (Thanksgiving) 是 ________ (date) __________(weekday) 。
5. 圣诞节 [Shèngdànjié] (Christmas) 是 __________ (date) __________ (weekday) 。
6. 我的生日是 __________ (date), 今年在 __________ (weekday) 。

B. Complete the following sentences with the help of the clues:

1. 下个星期日我要 ______________________________________。
(to hold a birthday party for my boyfriend)

2. 你可以 ______________________________________?
(to make an order of Chinese dumplings for me)

3. 后天是妈妈的生日，我要 ______________________________________。
(to buy a very pretty shirt for her)

IV. Comprehensive Exercises

Make a telephone call to your friend inviting him/her to attend your boyfriend's birthday party next Saturday. You will need to include (but are not limited to) the following words and expressions:

生日　空　晚会　月　号　还是　为　参加　知道　地址

____

____

____

____

____

____

____

____

Name: ________________ Date: ____________

Lesson 15 The Library Is in Front of the Dorm

I. Listening Exercises

A. Liang Zhi is giving you a brief introduction of his dorm. Listen carefully and then draw a floor plan based on what you hear:

B. Answer the following questions based on this floor plan:

1. 梁志的宿舍在哪儿?

____

2. 她的宿舍里边有什么?

____

3. 客厅的右边是什么?

____

4. 餐厅在厨房的哪边?

____

5. 宿舍的对面是什么?

____

II. Character Exercises

A. Circle characters that have both traditional and simplified forms. Write the traditional/simplified character pairs in the numbered spaces below the dialogue:

常飞：方园，你的宿舍在哪儿？

方园：我的宿舍在学校旁边。

常飞：你的宿舍有几个卧室？你有室友吗？

方园：有两个卧室。田真是我的室友。他的房间在右边，我的在左边。

常飞：你们宿舍有客厅吗？

方园：有一个客厅，还有一个餐厅。

常飞：有没有厨房？

方园：我们有厨房，是公用的。我们的宿舍很不错，你来看看吧。

1. ______ 2. ______ 3. ______ 4. ______ 5. ______ 6. ______

7. ______ 8. ______ 9. ______ 10. ______ 11. ______ 12. ______

13. ______ 14. ______ 15. ______ 16. ______ 17. ______

III. Grammar Exercises

A. Here is a floor plan of an apartment in the new dorm. Look at it and answer the following questions:

Note: 走廊 [zǒuláng]: hallway

厨房 餐厅

洗澡间

卧室

客厅

走廊#

前门

1. 卧室在哪儿?

____

2. 卧室的对面是什么?

____

3. 厨房和洗澡间的中间是什么?

____

4. 客厅和卧室的中间有什么?

____

5. 餐厅在客厅的哪边?

____

B. Fill in the blanks with 有，在，是 with the help of the pictures:

1. 

裙子 ______ 鞋的右边。

裙子的左边 ______ 鞋。

Notes: 右边 [yòubiān]: right
左边 [zuǒbiān]: left

2. 

房子的后边 ______ 一棵树。

房子 ______ 树的前边。

Notes: 棵 [kē]: measure word for plants
树 [shù]: tree

3. 

球的左边 ______ 一件衬衫，鞋 ______ 球的下边。

衬衫 ______ 球的左边，球的下边 ______ 鞋。

IV. Comprehensive Exercises

You are learning about housing in the U.S. Each of you is required to give a short talk to your class about your house. You are now preparing for the talk. Write out what you want to say in your introduction. Use as many words and expressions as possible from the text. The following expressions can be used as well:

大门	[dàmén]	main gate	楼梯	[lóutī]	stairs
车库	[chēkù]	garage	院子	[yuànzi]	(court)yard
地下室	[dìxiàshì]	basement			

____

____

____

____

Name: __________________ Date: ____________

Lesson 16 She Plays Basketball Very Well

I. Listening Exercises

A. Listen to the dialogue and fill in the blanks based on what you hear:

爱文：信美，你喜欢什么 __________？

信美：我喜欢打球。我 ______________________。

爱文：是吗？我也喜欢打球，可是我喜欢打排球。我排球 ____________。

信美：你 ______________ 怎么样？我 _________ 不太好。我得多练习练习。

爱文：我 ______________ 马马虎虎 [mǎmǎhūhū]。我也得多练习。

Notes: 运动 [yùndòng]: sports, exercises

马马虎虎 [mǎmǎhūhū]: just so-so

B. Listen to the sentences and choose the correct answer:

1. a. 小美做饭做得很慢。
   b. 小美吃饭吃得很慢。
2. a. 欢欢篮球打得不太好。
   b. 欢欢篮球打得太好了。
3. a. 正然作业做得很快、很好。
   b. 正然写字写得很好。

II. Character Exercises

A. Match the traditional form of the characters with their simplified forms:

鍛  籃  體 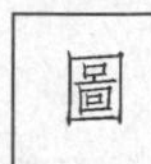 圖  邊  業  廳

篮  体  边  厅  图  锻  业

B. Find from the lesson the characters with the following radicals:

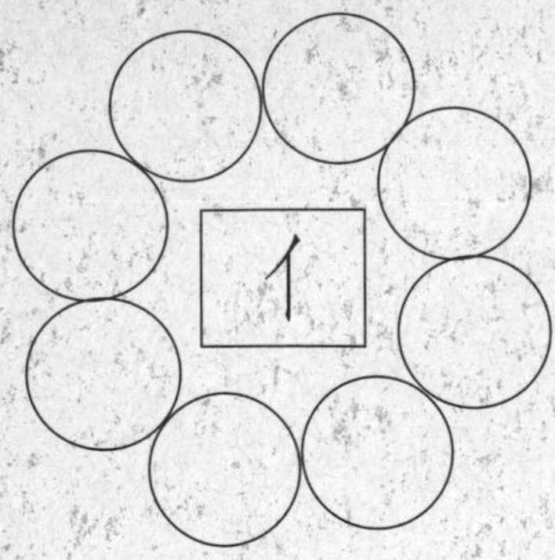

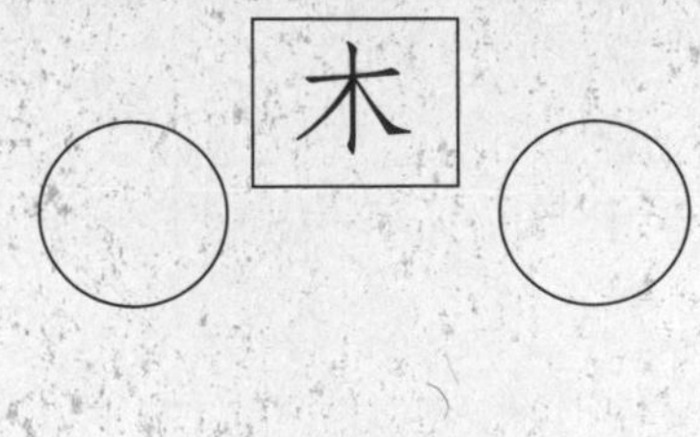

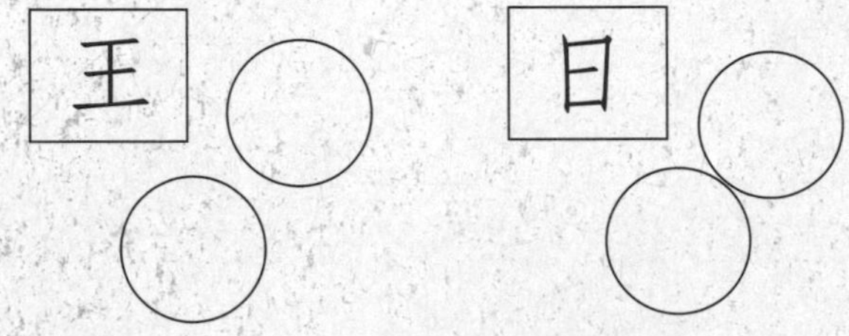

III. Grammar Exercises

A. Translate the following into Chinese:

1. He came very early.

____

2. I often eat very slowly.

____

3. You walk too fast.

____

4. He plays basketball very well.

____

5. My roommate goes to bed very late.

____

6. My mom makes dumplings very fast.

____

Name: ____________ Date: ____________

B. Rewrite the following sentences with emphasis on the object of each sentence:

1. 她打篮球打得不错。

____

2. 妈妈包饺子包得非常快。

____

3. 谁做饭做得很好?

____

4. 我睡觉睡得太少。

____

IV. Comprehensive Exercises

A. Read the following paragraph and then answer the questions. Look up the new words in a dictionary when needed:

包健和杨中是室友。他们俩都非常喜欢运动，常常一起去健身房锻炼。包健游泳游得特别好，他是学校游泳队的队长，他也是杨中的游泳教练。杨中游得也不错，可是他不常常游泳。

他喜欢打球，特别是篮球，他打得非常好，投球投得特别准。他也喜欢打排球、乒乓球。排球、乒乓球他都打得不错。他是学校篮球队的中锋，每次比赛他都要参加。

他们俩不但喜欢运动，而且还喜欢做饭。包健包饺子包得很快，也很好看。杨中做中国菜做得特别好吃。他们也常常请同学们去他们的宿舍吃饭。同学们常常吃得很多，吃得太饱了。

Notes: 队 [duì]: team
队长 [duìzhǎng]: team leader
特别 [tèbié]: especially
投 [tóu]: throw
准 [zhǔn]: accurate
乒乓球 [pīngpāngqiú]: table tennis
中锋 [zhōngfēng]: center (in basketball game)
不但……而且……[búdàn …… érqiě ……]: not only . . . but also . . .
饱 [bǎo]: full

Questions:

1. 包健和杨中常常去哪儿?

2. 包健什么特别好? 杨中呢?

3. 杨中喜欢什么运动?

4. 他们俩做饭做得怎么样?

5. 同学们常常去他们宿舍做什么?

B. Change the above paragraph into a dialogue between 包健 and 杨中:

Name: ________________ Date: ____________

Lesson 17 Spring Is Coming Soon

I. Listening Exercises

A. Listen and fill in the blanks, then translate them into English:

1. ___ ___ 就要来了，天气很快就要 ___ 了。

   ____

2. 有 ___ ___ 我会去 ___ ___ 玩玩。

   ____

3. 我很喜欢吃中国菜，___ ___ 我最喜欢吃牛肉面。

   ____

4. 这两天 ___ ___ ___，我想去游泳池游泳。你也去吗？

   ____

5. 我学习不太忙 ___ ___ ___，就跟你一起去看电影。

   ____

6. 这个学期就要 ___ 了，我们很快就要 ___ 春假了。

   ____

B. Listen to the dialogue between 夏华 and 春红, then mark the correct statements with "✓" and the incorrect ones with "✗":

☐ 1. 春红这个学期不忙。

☐ 2. 春红就要参加学校的篮球赛了。

☐ 3. 夏华在春假的时候要回家。

☐ 4. 夏华就要和她的好朋友见面了。

II. Character Exercises

A. Write out the characters for the following Pinyin:

1. chūntiān ______
2. qìhòu ______
3. dōngtiān ______
4. rèjíle ______
5. dù ______
6. fàngjià ______
7. nuǎnhuo ______
8. xiàyǔ ______
9. zuì ______
10. shíjiān ______
11. huáshì ______
12. xiàxuě ______
13. qízhōng ______
14. guāfēng ______
15. hǎojiǔbújiàn ______
16. jiànmiàn ______

B. Find the radicals in the following characters, indicate their numbers of strokes, and then write their definitions from an English dictionary:

Characters	Radical	No. of strokes	Definition
春	日	9	spring
夏			
秋			
冬			
气			
最			
暖			
热			
短			
度			
极			
风			
雪			

Name: ____________ Date: ____________

III. Grammar Exercises

A. Select an appropriate pattern from the list and place it correctly in the sentence:

……的时候，就要/快要……了，其中

1. 我有一辆白色的车。

____

2. 她的弟弟今年十八岁。

____

3. 这个学期我有五门课。我最喜欢中文课。

____

4. 开车不应该打手机。

____

B. Read the following passage and fill in the blanks with appropriate words or phrases:

下个月是三月，我们很快_____要_____春假了。春假的_____ _____，我和我的室友小玲要去加拿大的多伦多 [Duōlúnduō] (Toronto) 玩。明天下午我和小玲_____没有课，我们想一起去商店 [shāngdiàn] (store) 买要去加拿大穿的衣服。小玲说她想买一条裙子，我说不好。多伦多的三月_____ _____ _____会非常冷，最冷的_____ _____才华氏三十度，冷_____了。我说买一条牛仔裤怎么样，她说很好。我想买一_____鞋。商店里皮鞋、球鞋和靴子_____在减价 [jiǎnjià] (on sale)，_____ _____我最想买一双球鞋。我们很快就_____去旅行 [lǚxíng] (travel) 了，我高兴_____了！

C. Translate the following sentences into Chinese:

1. I will eat the Chinese food cooked by my mother soon.

   ____

2. They will attend the soccer game soon.

   ____

3. I like sports. Among the sports I like, I enjoy playing basketball the most.

   ____

4. Sometimes she uses chopsticks to eat.

   ____

5. This birthday cake is extremely delicious.

   ____

IV. Comprehensive Exercises

Write an essay describing the climate of the place where you come from (at least 100 characters).

Please include the following words and phrases:

……的时候，就要/快要……了，其中，最，极了，华氏/摄氏

____

____

____

____

____

____

Name: ____________ Date: ____________

Lesson 18 We Are Going to Take a Train Trip

I. Listening Exercises

A. Listen to the dialogue and read the statements below. Mark a "✓" for a correct statement and a "✗" for an incorrect one. Write out the correct answer for the wrong statement:

☐ 1. 文健春假要去看他的爷爷奶奶。 ____________

☐ 2. 小华春假要去佛罗里达。 ____________

☐ 3. 文健的爸爸妈妈住在洛杉矶。 ____________

☐ 4. 小华要和朋友一起开车去玩儿。 ____________

☐ 5. 文健和妹妹都喜欢去海边游泳。 ____________

Notes: 爷爷 [yéye]: grandpa
奶奶 [nǎinai]: grandma
佛罗里达 [Fóluólǐdá]: Florida

B. Listen to the questions and then give answers based on your actual situation:

1. ____________
2. ____________
3. ____________
4. ____________
5. ____________

II. Character Exercises

A. Listen to the above dialogue again and write it down in characters:

____

____

____

____

____

____

____

____

B. Read the dialogue you have written, circle all the characters that have a simplified/traditional form, and provide them below:

Example: 车 (車)

______ ______ ______ ______ ______ ______

______ ______ ______ ______ ______ ______

______ ______ ______ ______ ______

Name: ________________ Date: ____________

III. Grammar Exercises

A. Ask a question on each pair of words given below and then answer it according to the requirements for each sentence:

1. Use "离" *Requirement*

   Hint: 教室 [jiàoshì] classroom (健身房) (教室)

   ____

   ____

2. Talk about means of transportation *Requirement*

   Hint: 华盛顿 [Huáshèngdùn]: Washington (纽约) (华盛顿)

   ____

   ____

3. Indicating sequence *Requirement*

   Hint: 商店 [shāngdiàn]: retail store (商店) (公园)

   ____

   ____

4. Use "近" or "远" *Requirement*

   (图书馆) (停车场)

   ____

   ____

B. The following are the things 文健 is going to do tomorrow. Divide these things into three groups: things to be done in the morning, afternoon, and evening. Arrange them properly, put them into sentences, and then use 先, 再, and 然后 to connect them:

看朋友 游泳 做功课 去买东西 吃早饭
上课 上网 去图书馆 打电话

Note: 东西 [dōngxi]: things

C. Complete the following sentences with a verb phrase based on the artwork clues:

1. 从美国去中国，你得 ________________ 。

2. 春假她要 ___________ 回家看爸爸妈妈。

3. *A*: 我们怎么去这个饭馆?

   B: 我们坐 _________________ 去。

4. *A*: 你会 ________________ 吗?

   B: 不会。我会 _____________ 。

Name: ____________ Date: ____________

IV. Comprehensive Exercises

You are in the dorm chatting with your roommate about your plan for the coming summer. Write a paragraph about your plan beginning with the following sentence. You need to include where you are going, what you are going to do, and what transportation you will use.

我们就要放暑假了……

____

____

____

____

____

____

____

____

Name: ____________ Date: ____________

Lesson 19 I Caught a Cold

I. Listening Exercises

A. Listen to the dialogue between 黄飞 and 白雪, and mark the correct statements with "✓" and the incorrect ones with "✗":

☐ 1. 白雪来美国三个月了。

☐ 2. 白雪刚刚 [gāng gāng] (just; a short while ago) 来美国的时候喜欢吃美国菜。

☐ 3. 白雪生病以后去看医生了。

☐ 4. 白雪现在没有生病了。

☐ 5. 白雪现在不喜欢吃美国菜了。

☐ 6. 白雪现在还不会做美国菜。

B. Listen to the dialogue between 田小西 and 程小东, and mark the correct statements with "✓" and the incorrect ones with "✗":

☐ 1. 小东上个月买了一辆车。

☐ 2. 小西会开车。

☐ 3. 坐公共汽车要一个半小时才能到学校。

☐ 4. 小东说有时候开车只要五分钟就能到学校了。

II. Character Exercises

A. Write the characters for the following Pinyin:

1. hǎoxiàng
2. gǎnmào
3. bǐjì
4. fùxí
5. shūfu
6. zhǔnbèi
7. gǎnxiè
8. kǎoshì
9. suǒyǐ
10. yīshēng
11. chīyào
12. fāshāo
13. késòu
14. shēngbìng
15. xiūxi
16. tóuténg

B. Write the components of the following characters and circle the radical:

Example: 饿 ⓘ饣 + 我

1. 感 ____________________
2. 像 ____________________
3. 医 ____________________
4. 药 ____________________
5. 准 ____________________
6. 笔 ____________________
7. 复 ____________________
8. 发 ____________________

Name: __________________ Date: ____________

III. Grammar Exercises

A. Change the following sentences to questions, then give a negative answer to each question:

1. 这个夏天我就要去北京学中文了。

   Question: ______________________________

   Negative answer: ______________________________

2. 她做了两个蛋糕。

   Question: ______________________________

   Negative answer: ______________________________

3. 我下了课以后，就去图书馆看书。

   Question: ______________________________

   Negative answer: ______________________________

4. 昨天我在我朋友家喝了很多酒。

   Question: ______________________________

   Negative answer: ______________________________

B. Translate the following sentences into Chinese:

1. I bought that red skirt tonight.

   ____

2. Let's go swimming together after you recover from your illness.

   ____

3. I haven't eaten for the whole day today. Therefore, I feel very hungry now.

   ____

4. He has read three Chinese novels.

   ____

5. I traveled to the West during the spring break.

   ____

IV. Comprehensive Exercises

Guided composition:

You have been staying up very late for several days and have caught a cold. You felt too sick to attend Chinese class today. Please write an excuse note to the teacher. Your classmate will bring the note to your Chinese teacher.

Write the note according to the following format. (Write at least 80 characters)

_____老师：

____

____

____

____

____

____

____

____

学生：(你的名字)

(　　年　　月　　日)

Name: ________________ Date: ____________

Lesson 20 I've Brought Xiao Xie Over . . .

I. Listening Exercises

A. Listen and write the Pinyin for the following expressions:

1. 我想搬出去住。 ____________________
2. 我把我女朋友带来了。 ____________________
3. 每个月的第一天必须付房租。 ____________________
4. 请你马上下来。 ____________________

B. Listen to the dialogue and mark the correct statements with "✓" and the incorrect ones with "✗":

☐ 1. 那是小明的公寓，他们先在外面，然后进去。

☐ 2. 那是小明的电视，他从家里搬过来的。

☐ 3. 小谢把房租带来了。

☐ 4. 房东太太住在楼上。

☐ 5. 小明跑上楼去把中文书给房东太太。

II. Character Exercises

A. For each character, make two phrases, write down the Pinyin, and make a few sentences:

搬	搬下去 搬下来	bānshàngqù bānxiàlái	你想把桌子搬下去吗? 是的，我想把桌子搬下来。
带			
楼			
烟			

B. Write down the radical of each of the following characters and provide the meaning of the radical. List at least five characters that have the same radical:

Example: 吗　口　mouth　呢　喝　吃　和　啊

1. 回 ______________________________

2. 搬 ______________________________

3. 饭 ______________________________

4. 但 ______________________________

5. 楼 ______________________________

III. Grammar Exercises

A. <u>**Situation:**</u> 明学's Mom is coming to visit him the day after tomorrow. This is their phone conversation.

1. Fill in the blanks with 把 and a directional complement:

明学：喂，是妈妈吗？我是明学。你后天_____ 我的车_____ _____ _____ 的时候 (drive my car over)，也_____ 我的电脑_____ _____ _____ (move my computer over)，好吗？

妈妈：可以，要不要也_____ 你的夏天衣服_____ _____ _____ (bring your summer clothes over) 呢？

明学：也好，一定要_____ 那件黄衬衫_____ _____ _____ (bring it over)，我很喜欢那件。

妈：没问题。噢！对了，爸爸给你买了一个新手机。

明学：太好了！请_____ 那个新手机也_____ _____ _____ (bring it over) 给我吧！

妈： 我今天做了饺子，要不要也 _____ 一些 _____ _____ (bring some over) 呢？

明学：太好了，我的室友要 _____ _____ _____ 了 (move out)，他很喜欢吃饺子，你多拿一些 _____ _____ (take some over)，可以请他也尝尝 [chángchang] (have a taste of)。

妈： 那我就多 _____ 一 些 _____ _____ (take some over)。

明学：妈，我好困 [kùn] (sleepy) 哦！(I am very sleepy!) 我想再回 _____ (go back) 睡觉。

妈： 你昨天晚上是什么时候从学校回 _____ (go back) 的？

明学：我没有车，我是 _____ _____ _____ 的 (walk back)，十一点半才 _____ _____ (come back)。再见！

B. Answer the following questions in Chinese (use 把 and/or directional complements):

1. 明学的妈妈什么时候过去看他？

____

2. 妈妈要带什么过去？

____

3. 明学要妈妈把黄衬衫怎么样？

____

4. 新手机是谁买的？要怎么处理 [chǔlǐ] (deal with) 呢？

____

5. 明学昨天晚上是什么时候回去的？

____

IV. Comprehensive Exercises

Translate the following passage into English (paying attention to the usage of 把 and directional complements).

刻舟求剑 [kè zhōu qiú jiàn]
(Mark the boat to find the sword)

有一个楚国人 (the State of Chu)，他坐船 (boat) 要到河的对面去的时候，一不小心 (due to carelessness)，他的剑 (sword) 从他身上掉下去了。

他想把剑捡回来，可是剑已经 (already) 掉进河里去了，怎么办呢? (What should we do?) 那个楚国人，赶快 (hurry) 要他的仆人 (servant) 把他的刀子 (knife) 拿过来，他在船的旁边刻上 (carve) 了一个记号 (mark)。

有人问他：你怎么不下去把剑拿上来呢？为什么 (why) 在船旁边刻上 (carve) 一个记号 (mark)呢？那个楚国人指著 (point at) 记号回答 (reply)说：我的剑是从刻这个记号的地方掉下去的，下次我到这儿来的时候，在记号的地方跳下去，就可以把我的剑捞 (scoop up) 上来了。

English translation:

Name: ____________________ Date: ______________

Lesson 21 What Will You Do During the Summer Vacation?

I. Listening Exercises

Listen and answer in Chinese characters:

1. ______________________________

2. ______________________________

3. ______________________________

4. ______________________________

II. Character Exercises

A. For each character, make two phrases, write down the Pinyin, and make a few sentences.

业	毕业 作业	bìyè zuòyè	你今年夏天就要毕业了，对不对？ 我室友常一面做作业一面上网。
班			
打			
假			

B. Write down the radical of each of the following characters and provide the meaning of the radical. List at least five characters that have the same radical:

Example:

Characters	Radical	Meaning of radical	More characters
吗	口	mouth	呢 喝 吃 和 啊
留			
决			
找			
实			
运			

III. Grammar Exercises

Try to state at least six activities by using the following expressions:

(一面……一面…… / 一边……一边……)

我常……

我也喜欢……

Name: ________________ Date: ____________

IV. Comprehensive Exercises

Guided composition: Talk about your plan.

Requirements:

1. *Topic*: Talk about your plans for this summer or for after graduation.
2. Use at least 6 grammar points from the following:

   一面……一面…… / 一边……一边……；了；不……了；就要……了；正在……；然后；以前；以后；得；想；要；会；应该；觉得；把，etc.
3. Write at least 20 sentences.

____

____

____

____

____

____

____

____

Name: ____________ Date: ____________

Lesson 22 I Have Arrived in Shanghai

I. Listening Exercises

A. Listen and mark the correct statements with "✓" and the incorrect ones with "✗":

☐ 1. 我觉得上海的生活很有意思。

☐ 2. 我每天九点起床。

☐ 3. 我的中文老师常常请我去她家玩。

☐ 4. 我常常帮助我的朋友们学中文。

☐ 5. 我们每天要去参观上海的一些地方。

☐ 6. 我的朋友们喜欢每个星期三唱歌。

☐ 7. 上海有很多小吃 [xiǎochī] (snacks)。

☐ 8. 下个星期我们要去美国实习了。

☐ 9. 公司的老板是美国人。

☐ 10. 我们都一定努力工作，多学习。

II. Character Exercises

A. Find five words from the lesson for each of the following categories and write them in characters:

1. People or things

2. Action

3. Time words

4. Descriptive expressions

B. Find one word from each category of Exercise A, then put the words together to make a sentence. If necessary, you may use the word more than once.

1. ______________________________

2. ______________________________

3. ______________________________

4. ______________________________

5. ______________________________

III. Grammar Exercises

A. Find an appropriate measure word from the right column for the phrases in the left column and insert:

一_____ 报纸	一下儿
两_____ 运动衫	盘
三_____ 电脑公司	本
四_____ 城市	只
五_____ 课	一点儿
六_____ 炒面	件
七_____ 客人	双
八_____ 汉语书	家
九_____ 小狗	门
十_____ 筷子	一会儿
写_______ 汉字	张
看_______ 电视	位
我来介绍_______	个

Note: 一会儿 [yíhuèr]: a short while

Name: ____________ Date: ____________

B. Choose an appropriate conjunction from the following list for each sentence below:

和	还是	因为	可是	不过
虽然	或者	但是	所以	然后

1. 程程到上海已经一个星期了，他还没有给他女朋友打电话。

____

2. 他的公司的老板很不错，他很喜欢在这儿工作。

____

3. 今年暑假你想去北京的暑期班学习吗？你要去上海的公司实习吗？

____

4. 大明最喜欢喝绿茶可乐。

____

5. 方文春假想先坐火车再开车去洛杉矶看他的爷爷奶奶。

____

6. 我的车是手排挡的，你会开，没问题。

____

C. Tell your friend what you like about your university, using 比如 for details, talking about:

1. Your classes.

____

2. Your fellow students.

____

3. The restaurants near the university.

____

IV. Comprehensive Exercises

Guided composition:

You are now studying Chinese in a summer program in Shanghai/Beijing. You are staying at the dorm for foreign students. You have a room of your own. This is the third day after your arrival there. You are writing an email to your parents about your life and studies there. Because this is the first time you are abroad, your parents are very concerned about you. Therefore, you need to provide as many details as possible.

爸爸、妈妈：

我到北京/上海已经三天了。我在这儿都很好，我住在 ......

1 2 3 4 5 6 吗 ①

吗 ②

嗎 ③

ma: (Part.)
你是学生吗？ ④

kǒu 口
⑥ mouth

⑦ 吗 吗

⑧

丨 ⑤ ㄇ 口 口ㄱ 吗 吗

Guide for Students

1) Character with its stroke order indicated by numbers

2) Simplified form of the character

3) Traditional form of the character

4) Pinyin pronunciation, grammatical usage, and example sentence or phrase

5) Stroke order illustrated by writing the character progressively

6) Radical of the character with its Pinyin pronunciation and meaning

7) Ghosted images for students to trace over

8) Dotted graph lines to aid students' practice

Name: ____________ Date: ____________

Lesson 1 Hello!

你	你	你	nǐ: you 你好！	rén 人(亻) person
丿 亻 亻' 亻⺈ 伱 伱 你				

好	好	好	hǎo: good 你好！	nǚ 女 female
㇛ 女 女 女' 好 好				

是	是	是	shì: to be 我是学生。	rì 日 sun
丨 冂 日 日 旦 早 早 昰 是				

学	学	學	xué: (学生: student) 学生	zǐ 子 child
丶 ⺍ ⺍ ⺍ 𭕄 学 学 学				

生	生	生	shēng: (学生: student) 学生	shēng 生 produce
丿 ⺊ 𠂉 牛 生				

吗	吗	嗎	ma: (Part.) 你是学生吗？	kǒu 口 mouth
丨 口 口 口 吗 吗				

我	我	我	wǒ: I, me 我是学生。	gē 戈 spear
丿 二 手 手 我 我 我				

呢	呢	呢	ne: (Part.) 你呢？	kǒu 口 mouth
丨 口 口 口 口 呎 呎 呢				

也	也	也	yě: also, too 我也是学生。	yǐ 乙 second
乛 𠃌 也				

他	他	他	tā: he, him 他是学生。	rén 人(亻) person
丿 亻 仁 仲 他				

不	不	不	bù: no, not 不是	yī 一 one
一 ブ 才 不				

Name: ____________________ Date: ______________

老	老	老	lǎo: (老师: teacher) 老师	lǎo 耂 old
一	十	土	耂	耂 老

师	师	師	shī: (老师: teacher) 老师	jīn 巾 napkin
丨	刂	刂	帀	师

学	学	学	学	学	学	学	学	学	学
您	您	您	您	您	您	您	您	您	您
贵	贵	贵	贵	贵	贵	贵	贵	贵	贵

姓	姓	姓	姓	姓	姓	姓	姓	姓	姓
请	请	请	请	请	请	请	请	请	请
问	问	问	问	问	问	问	问	问	问

呢	呢	呢	呢	呢	呢	呢	呢	呢	呢
吗	吗	吗	吗	吗	吗	吗	吗	吗	吗
是	是	是	是	是	是	是	是	是	是

我	我	我	我	我	我	我	我	我	我
老	老	老	老	老	老	老	老	老	老
师	师	师	师	师	师	师	师	师	师

Name: ____________________ Date: ______________

Lesson 2 What's Your Surname?

Character	Simplified	Traditional	Meaning	Radical
您	您	您	nín: (for politeness) you 您好	xīn 心 (忄) heart
贵	贵	貴	guì: noble, honored; expensive 您贵姓?	bèi 貝 shell
姓	姓	姓	xìng: family name 我姓李。	nǚ 女 female
请	请	請	qǐng: please (请问: May I ask...) 请问	yán 言 (讠) word
问	问	問	wèn: ask (请问: May I ask...) 请问	mén 門 (门) door

的
de: (Part.)
我的名字
bái 白
white
英
Yīng: English
英文
cǎo 艸 (艹)
grass
文
wén:
language, writing
中文
wén 文
literature
名
míng: name
名字
kǒu 口
mouth
字
zì: character, word
(名字 míngzi: name)
名字
zǐ 子
child
中
zhōng:
(中文: Chinese;
中国: China)
中文 中国
gǔn 丨
down stroke

Name: ____________ Date: ____________

叫	叫	叫	jiào: to call 我叫小美	kǒu 口 mouth

什	什	什	shén: (什么 : what) 什么	rén 人 (亻) person

么	么	麼	me: (什么 : what) 什么	piě 丿 left slanted stroke

她	她	她	tā: she, her 她呢？	nǚ 女 female

谁	谁	誰	shéi: who, whom 她是谁？	yán 言 (讠) word

同	同	同	tóng: same, similar (同学 : classmate) 同学	kǒu 口 mouth

您您您您您您您您您您
贵贵贵贵贵贵贵贵贵贵
姓姓姓姓姓姓姓姓姓姓

请请请请请请请请请请
问问问问问问问问问问
的的的的的的的的的的

英英英英英英英英英英
文文文文文文文文文文
名名名名名名名名名名

字字字字字字字字字字
中中中中中中中中中中
叫叫叫叫叫叫叫叫叫叫

Name: ____________________ Date: ______________

Lesson 3 Which Country Are You From?

Character	Simplified	Traditional	Meaning	Radical
哪	哪	哪	nǎ: which 哪国人	kǒu 口 mouth
国	国	國	guó: country 美国	wéi 囗 enclosure
人	人	人	rén: person 中国人	rén 人 (亻) person
很	很	很	hěn: very 很好	chì 彳 step
对	对	對	duì: correct 对了。	cùn 寸 inch

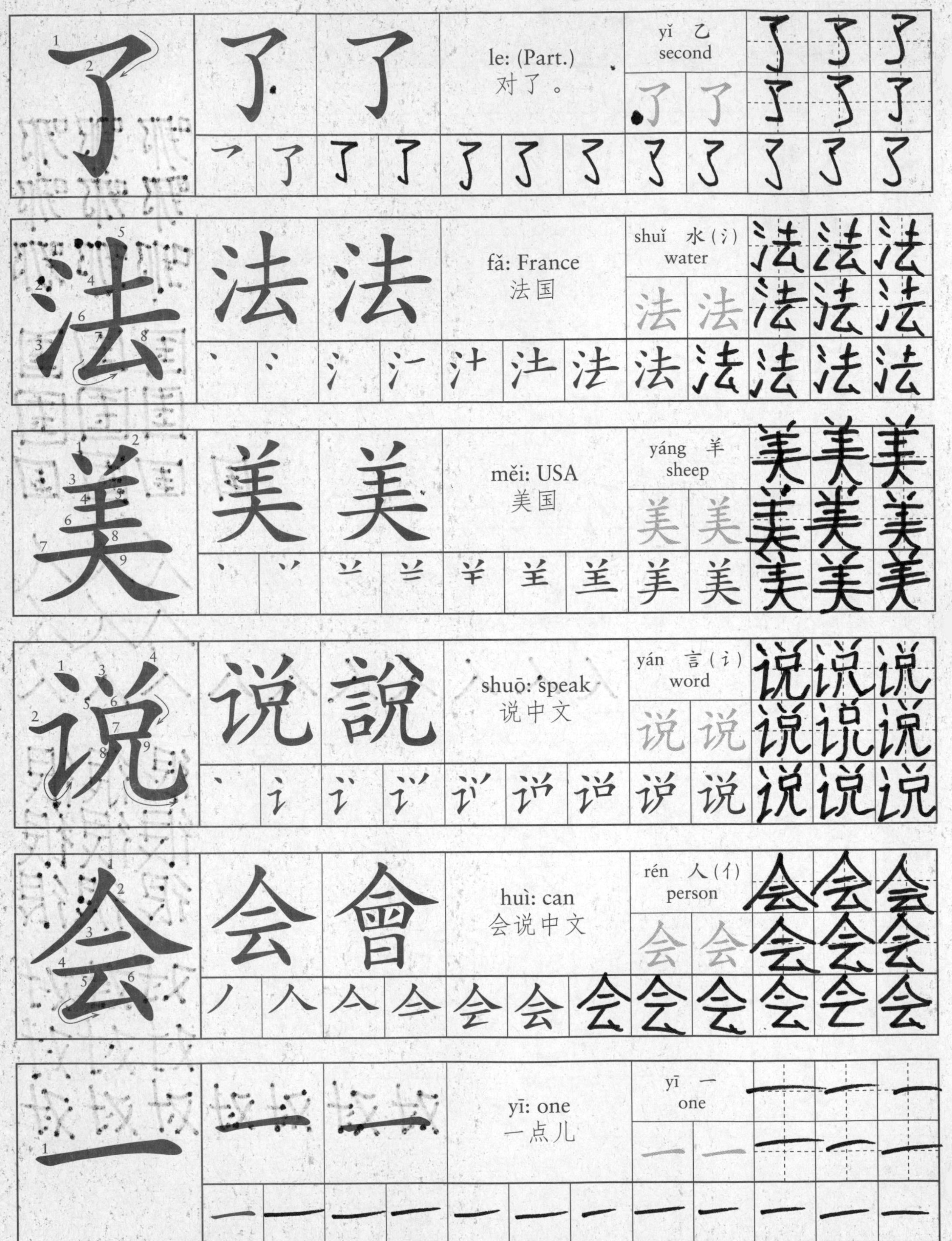
了 了
le: (Part.)
对了。
yǐ 乙
second
法 法
fǎ: France
法国
shuǐ 水 (氵)
water
美 美
měi: USA
美国
yáng 羊
sheep
说 說
shuō: speak
说中文
yán 言 (讠)
word
会 會
huì: can
会说中文
rén 人 (亻)
person
一 一
yī: one
一点儿
yī 一
one

Name: ______________ Date: ______________

点	点	點	diǎn: dot 一点儿	huǒ 火 (灬) fire
丨 ⺊ 占 点				

儿	儿	兒	ér: (retroflex ending) (一点儿: a little bit) 一点儿	ér 儿 walking man
丿 儿				

和	和	和	hé: and 我和你	kǒu 口 mouth
一 二 千 禾 和				

Name: ____________ Date: ____________

Lesson 4 What Do You Study?

Character	Simplified	Traditional	Meaning	Radical
那	那	那	nà: that 那是	yì 邑 (阝) city
书	书	書	shū: book 英文书	gǔn 丨 down stroke
这	这	這	zhè: this 这是	chuò 辵 (辶) motion
本	本	本	běn: (M.W.) 一本书	mù 木 wood
工	工	工	gōng: work (工程: engineering) 工程	gōng 工 work

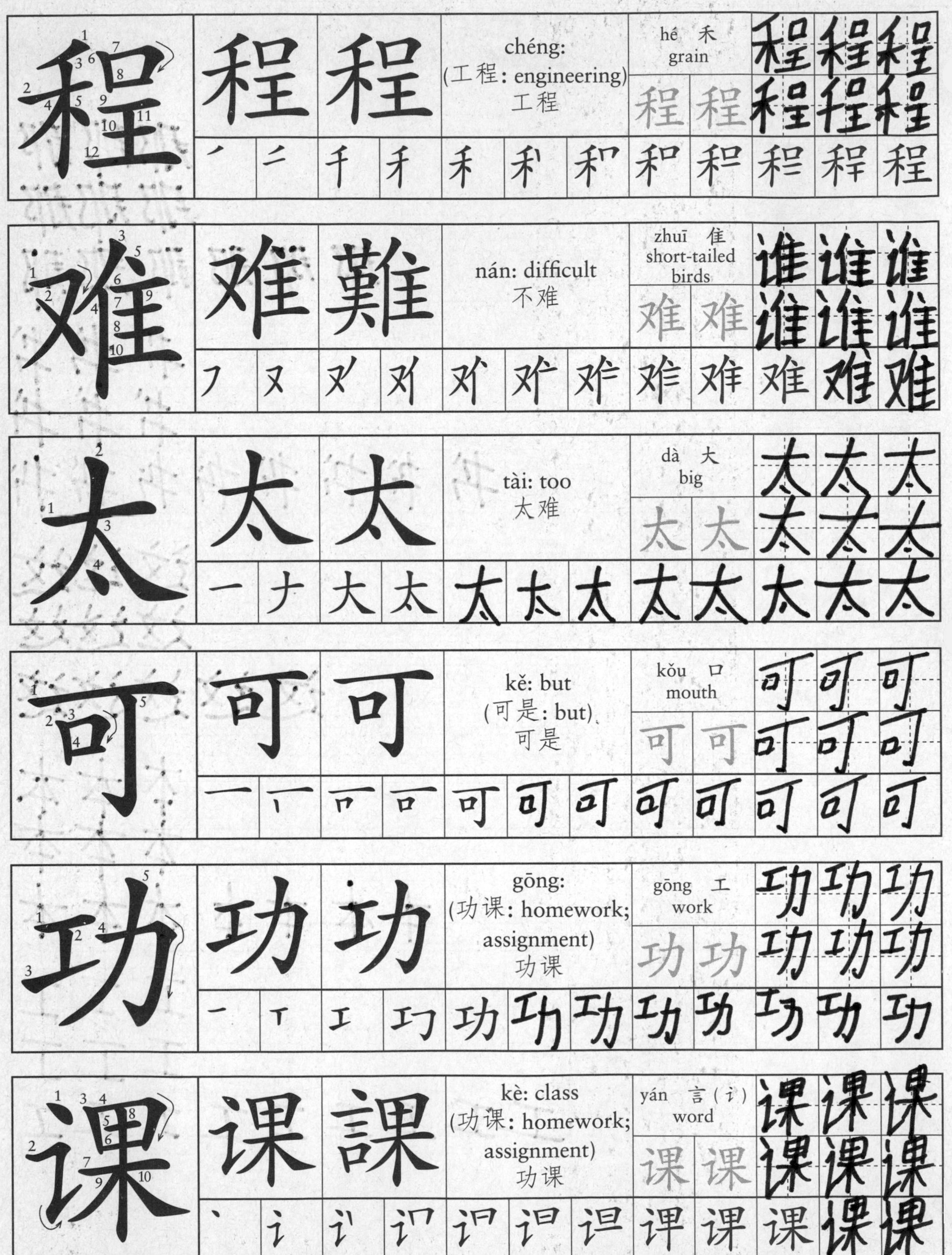
程 程 程
chéng:
(工程: engineering)
工程
hé 禾
grain
难 難
nán: difficult
不难
zhuī 隹
short-tailed birds
太 太 太
tài: too
太难
dà 大
big
可 可 可
kě: but
(可是: but)
可是
kǒu 口
mouth
功 功 功
gōng:
(功课: homework; assignment)
功课
gōng 工
work
课 課
kè: class
(功课: homework; assignment)
功课
yán 言 (讠)
word

Name: ____________ Date: ____________

多 — duō: many, much
很多
xī 夕 night

Stroke order: 丿 ㄅ 夕 多 多 多

们 們 — men: (used after a personal pronoun or a noun to show plural number); (他们: they)
我们
rén 人(亻) person

Stroke order: 丿 亻 亻 们 们

少 — shǎo: few, little
不少
xiǎo 小 small

Stroke order: 丨 小 小 少

gong

shao

men

duo

zhe

程	程	程	程	程	程	程	程	程	程
难	难	难	难	难	难	难	难	难	难
太	太	太	太	太	太	太	太	太	太

可	可	可	可	可	可	可	可	可	可
功	功	功	功	功	功	功	功	功	功
课	课	课	课	课	课	课	课	课	课

多	多	多	多	多	多	多	多	多	多
们	们	们	们	们	们	们	们	们	们
少	少	少	少	少	少	少	少	少	少

点	点	点	点	点	点	点	点	点	点
这	这	这	这	这	这	这	这	这	这
书	书	书	书	书	书	书	书	书	书

Name: ____________ Date: ____________

Lesson 5 This Is My Friend

Character	Simplified	Traditional	Meaning	Radical	Stroke order
朋	朋	朋	péng: friend (朋友: friend) 朋友	ròu 肉 (月) meat	丿 刀 月 月 月丿 朋 朋 朋
友	友	友	yǒu: friend (朋友 péngyou: friend) 朋友	yòu 又 right hand	一 ナ 方 友
来	来	來	lái: come 我来介绍一下。	yī 一 one	一 一 丆 丌 平 来 来
介	介	介	jiè: (介绍: introduce) 介绍	rén 人 (亻) person	丿 人 介 介
绍	绍	紹	shào: (介绍: introduce) 介绍	mì 糸 (纟) silk	𠃋 纟 纟 纫 纫 绍 绍 绍

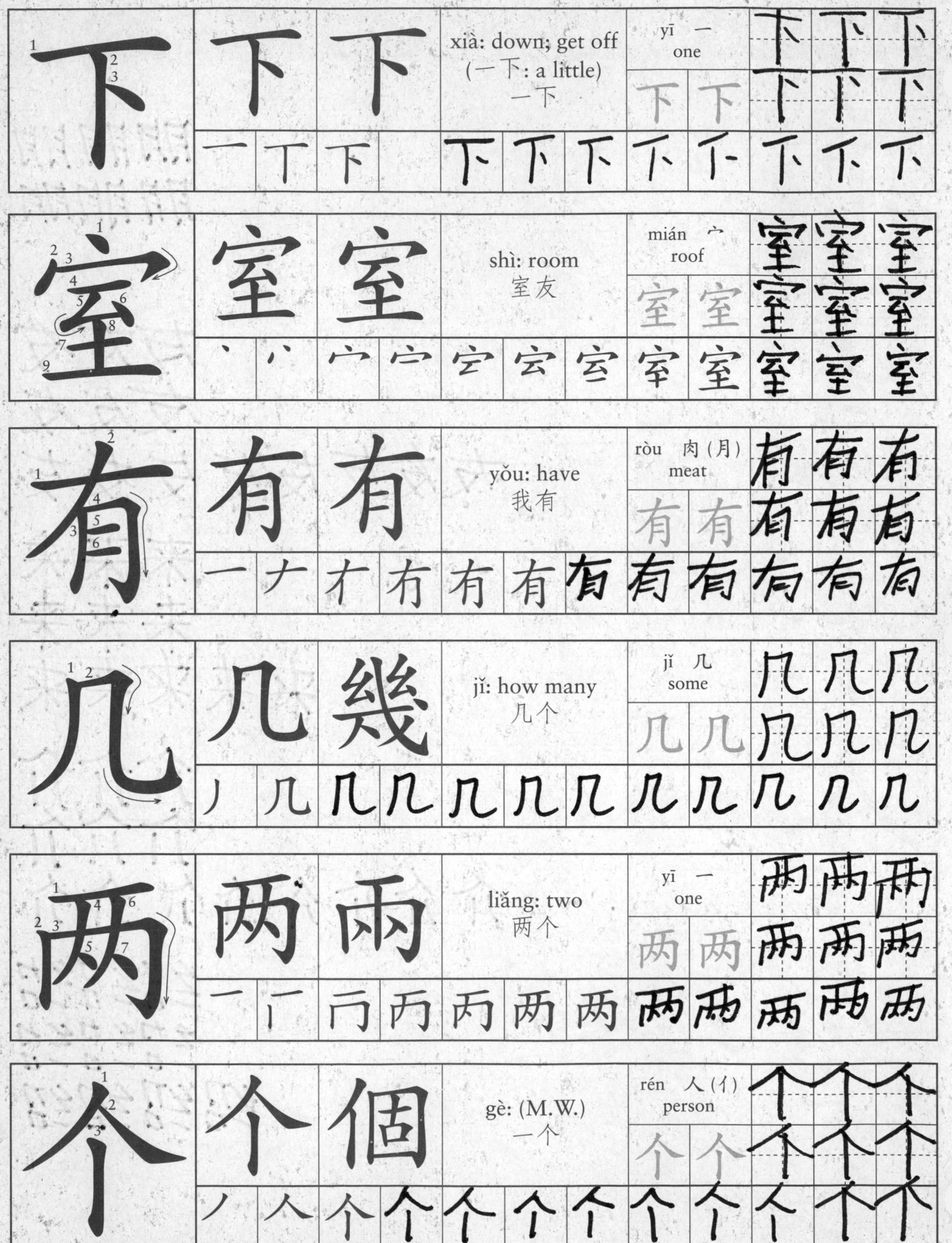

下
xià: down; get off
(一下: a little)
一下
yī 一
one
室
shì: room
室友
mián 宀
roof
有
yǒu: have
我有
ròu 肉 (月)
meat
几 幾
jǐ: how many
几个
jǐ 几
some
两 兩
liǎng: two
两个
yī 一
one
个 個
gè: (M.W.)
一个
rén 人 (亻)
person

Name: ____________________ Date: ______________

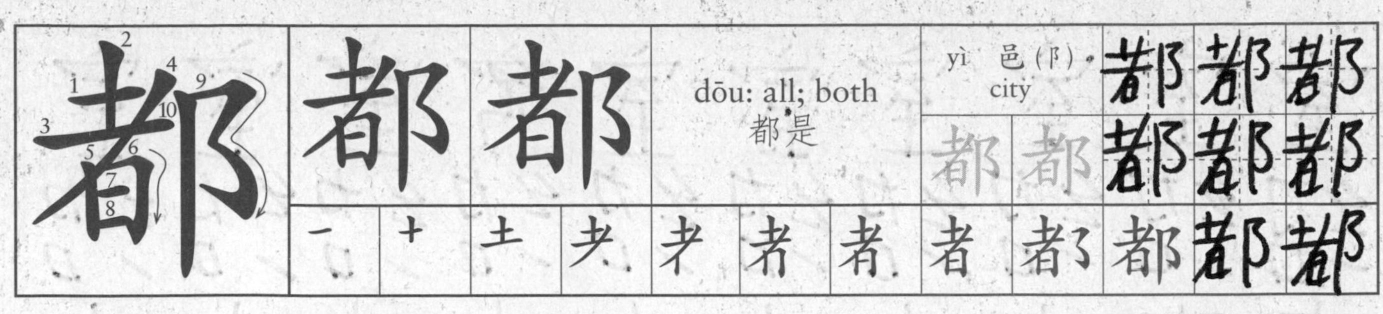

都
dōu: all; both
都是
yì 邑(阝)
city

常
cháng: often
常说中文
jīn 巾
napkin

跟
gēn: with
跟他
zú 足
foot

室室室室室室室室室室
绍绍绍绍绍绍绍绍绍绍
来来来来来来来来来来

友友友友友友友友友友
朋朋朋朋朋朋朋朋朋朋
个个个个个个个个个个

下下下下下下下下下下
几几几几几几几几几几
常常常常常常常常常常

都都都都都都都都都都
介介介介介介介介介介
介介介介介介介介介介

Name: ____________ Date: ____________

Lesson 6 My Family

Character	Simplified	Traditional	Meaning	Radical
家	家	家	jiā: home (大家: all; everybody) 我的家	mián 宀 roof
大	大	大	dà: big (大家: all; everybody) 大家	dà 大 big
从	从	從	cóng: from 从中国来	rén 人(亻) person
在	在	在	zài: at; in 在美国	tǔ 土 earth
四	四	四	sì: four 四个	wéi 口 enclosure

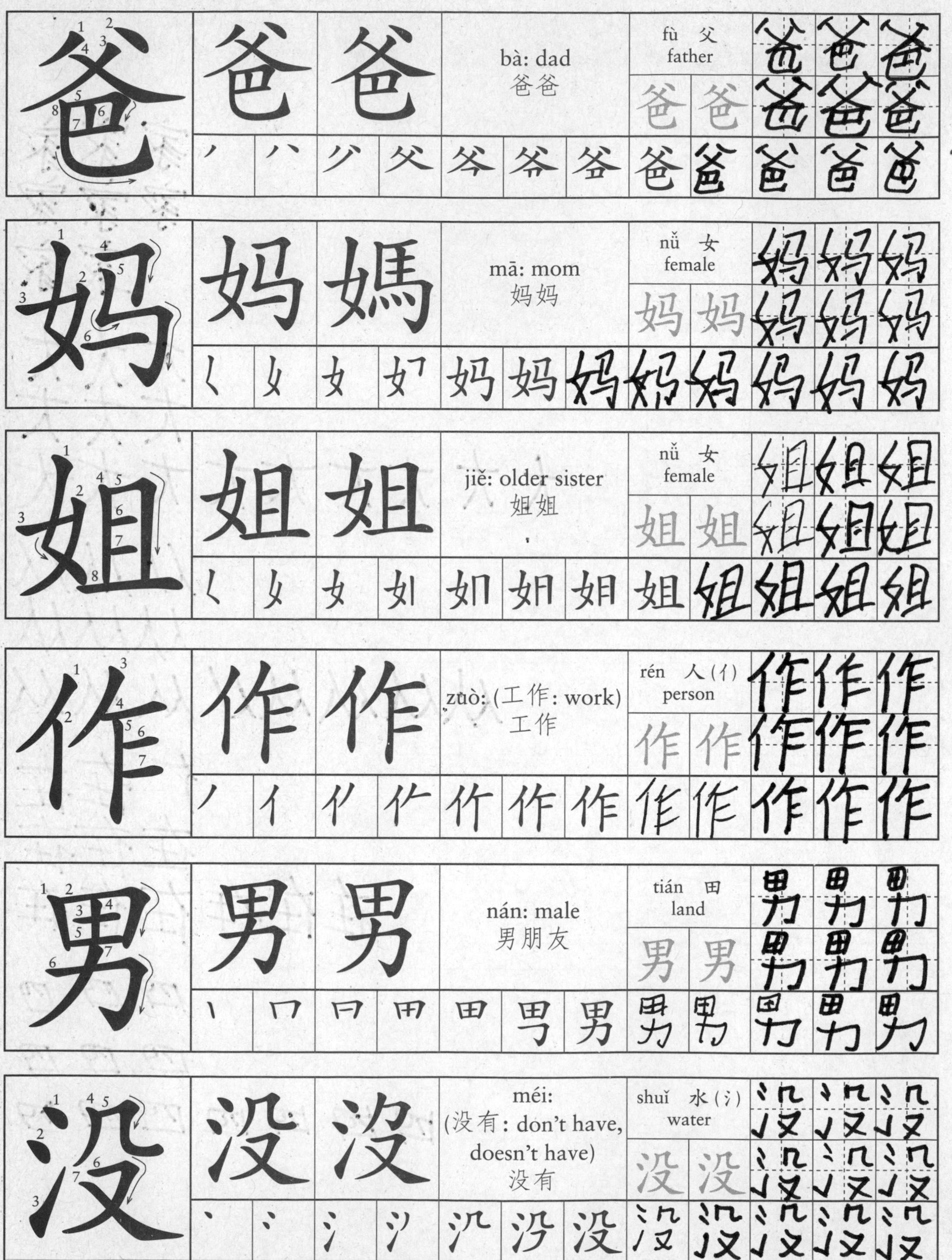
爸
bà: dad
爸爸
fù 父
father
妈 媽
mā: mom
妈妈
nǚ 女
female
姐
jiě: older sister
姐姐
nǚ 女
female
作
zuò: (工作: work)
工作
rén 人(亻)
person
男
nán: male
男朋友
tián 田
land
没
méi:
(没有: don't have,
doesn't have)
没有
shuǐ 水(氵)
water

辆	辆	輛	liàng: (measure word for vehicles) 两辆车	chē 車 (车) vehicle
车	车	車	chē: car 美国车	chē 車 (车) vehicle
只	只	隻	zhī: (M.W.) 一只狗	kǒu 口 mouth
狗	狗	狗	gǒu: dog 一只狗	quǎn 犬 (犭) one
爱	爱	愛	ài: love 我爱我的家。	zhǎo 爪 (爫) claw

家家家家家家家家家家
大大大大大大大大大大
从从从从从从从从从从

在在在在在在在在在在
四四四四四四四四四四
爸爸爸爸爸爸爸爸爸爸

妈妈妈妈妈妈妈妈妈妈
姐姐姐姐姐姐姐姐姐姐
作作作作作作作作作作

男男男男男男男男男男
没没没没没没没没没没
辆辆辆辆辆辆辆辆辆辆

Name: ____________ Date: ____________

Lesson 7 Where Do You Live?

Character			Meaning	Radical
住	住	住	zhù: live 住在	rén 人(亻) person
宿	宿	宿	sù: put up for the night (宿舍: dorm) 宿舍	mián 宀 roof
舍	舍	舍	shè: house (宿舍: dorm) 宿舍	rén 人(亻) person
号	号	號	hào: number 号码	kǒu 口 mouth
房	房	房	fáng: house 房间	hù 户 door

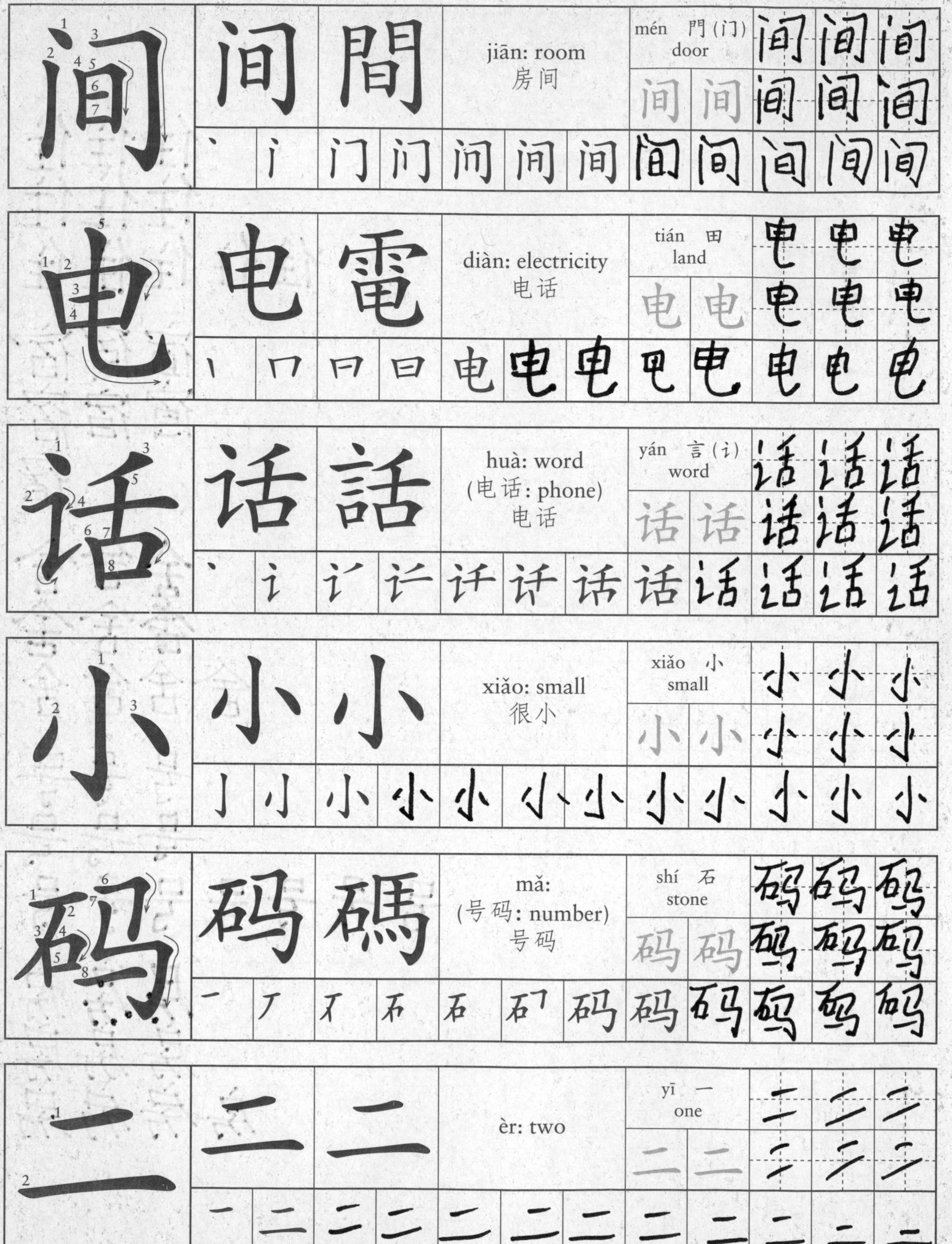

间 間
jiān: room
房间
mén 門(门)
door
电 電
diàn: electricity
电话
tián 田
land
话 話
huà: word
(电话: phone)
电话
yán 言(讠)
word
小 小
xiǎo: small
很小
xiǎo 小
small
码 碼
mǎ:
(号码: number)
号码
shí 石
stone
二 二
èr: two
yī 一
one

Name: ____________________ Date: ______________

三	三	三	sān: three	yī 一 one

五	五	五	wǔ: five	yī 一 one

六	六	六	liù: six	tóu 亠 cover

七	七	七	qī: seven	yī 一 one

八	八	八	bā: eight	bā 八 eight

九	九	九	jiǔ: nine	yǐ 乙 second

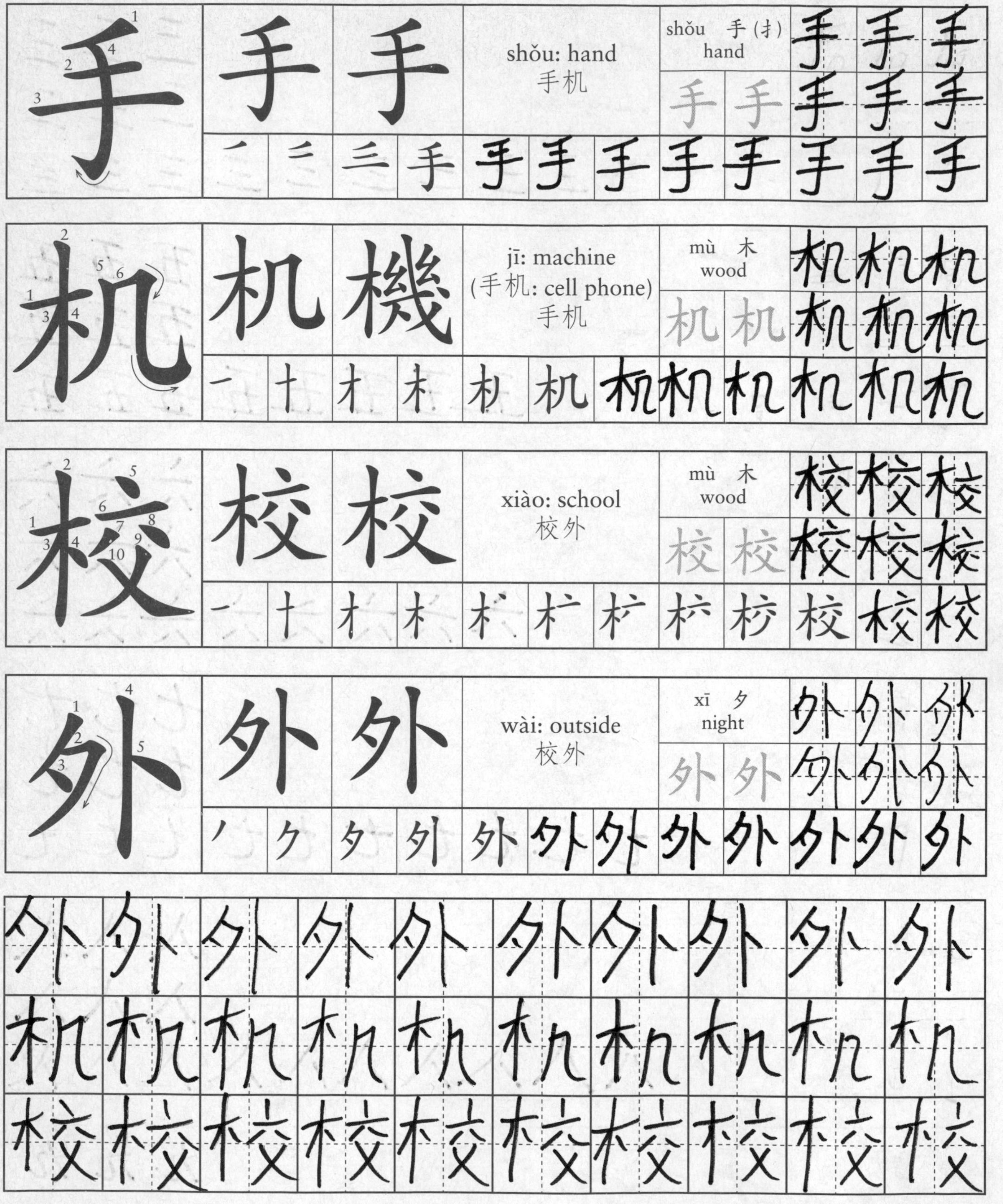
手
手 手
shǒu: hand
手机
shǒu 手 (扌)
hand
机
机 機
jī: machine
(手机: cell phone)
手机
mù 木
wood
校
校 校
xiào: school
校外
mù 木
wood
外
外 外
wài: outside
校外
xī 夕
night

Name: ____________ Date: ____________

Lesson 8 Do You Know Him?

Character	Simplified	Traditional	Meaning	Radical
认	认	認	rèn: (认识: know, recognize) 认识	yán 言(讠) word
识	识	識	shí: (认识 rènshi: know, recognize) 认识	yán 言(讠) word
去	去	去	qù: go 去哪儿	sī 厶 private; cocoon
上	上	上	shàng: get on, go to (上课: attend class) 上课	yī 一 one
以	以	以	yǐ: (以后: after, later) 以后	rén 人(亻) person

后
后 後
hòu: behind
(以后: after; later)
以后
kǒu 口
mouth
事
事 事
shì: matter, thing, business
事儿
yī 一
one
想
想 想
xiǎng: want
我想
xīn 心(忄)
heart
回
回 回
huí: return
回宿舍
wéi 口
enclosure
起
起 起
qǐ:
(一起: together)
一起
zǒu 走
walk
吃
吃 吃
chī: eat
吃饭
kǒu 口
mouth

Name: ____________ Date: ____________

饭	饭	飯	fàn: meal 吃饭	shí 食(饣) food

丿 ⺈ 饣 饣 饤 饭 饭

菜	菜	菜	cài: dish 日本菜	cǎo 艸(艹) grass

今	今	今	jīn: (今天: today) 今天	rén 人(亻) person

丿 人 亽 今

天	天	天	tiān: day 今天	yī 一 one

一 二 チ 天

次	次	次	cì: order, sequence (下次: next time) 下次	qiàn 欠 owe

丶 冫 冫 次 次 次

怎	怎	怎	zěn: (怎么样: how) 怎么样	xīn 心(忄) heart

丿 𠂉 亇 乍 乍 乍 怎 怎 怎

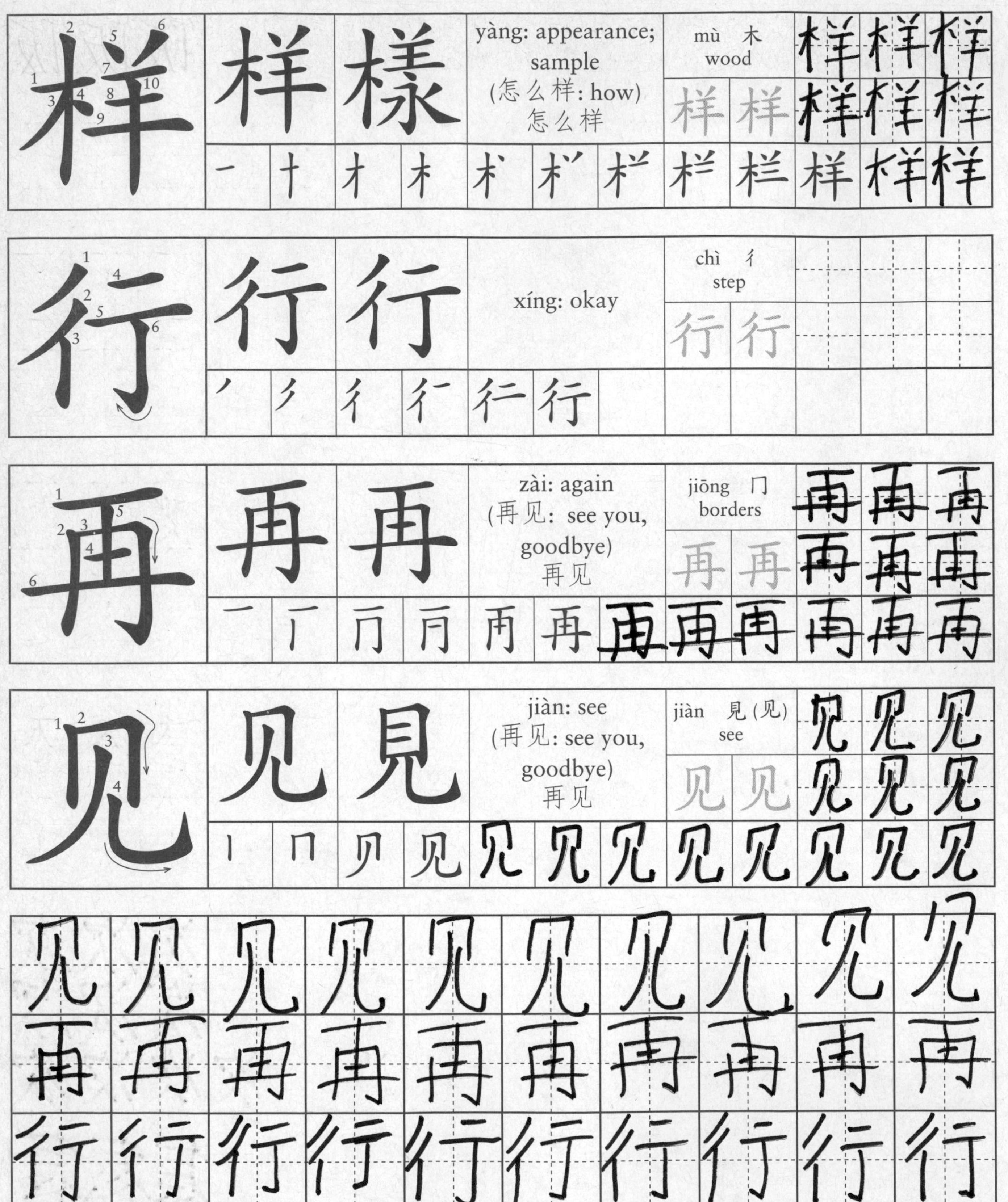
样
樣
yàng: appearance; sample
(怎么样: how)
怎么样
mù 木
wood
行
xíng: okay
chì 彳
step
再
zài: again
(再见: see you, goodbye)
再见
jiōng 冂
borders
见
見
jiàn: see
(再见: see you, goodbye)
再见
jiàn 見 (见)
see

Name: ____________________ Date: ______________

Lesson 9 He Is Making a Phone Call

Character	Meaning	Radical	Stroke order
打	dǎ: hit; play (打电话: make a phone call) 打电话	shǒu 手 (扌) hand	一 扌 扌 扌 打
喂	wèi (wéi): hello, hey	kǒu 口 mouth	口 口 口 口 口 口 口 口 口 喂
等	děng: wait 等一下儿	zhú 竹 (⺮) bamboo	丿 𠂉 ⺮ ⺮ ⺮ ⺮ 笁 笁 笁 笁 等 等
知	zhī: know 知道	shǐ 矢 arrow	丿 𠂉 𠂉 午 矢 知
道	dào: road; talk (知道: know) 知道	chuò 辵 (辶) motion	丶 丷 丷 丷 丷 丷 丷 首 首 道

谢	谢	謝	xiè: thanks 谢谢	yán 言 (讠) word 谢 谢
	丶 讠 讠 讠 访 讷 询 询 谕 谢 谢 谢			

吧	吧	吧	ba: (Part.) 你是小美吧？	kǒu 口 mouth 吧 吧
	口 叮 叩 吧 吧			

忙	忙	忙	máng: busy 很忙	xīn 心 (忄) heart 忙 忙
	丶 丷 忄 忄 忙 忙			

正	正	正	zhèng: in process of 正在	zhǐ 止 stop 正 正
	一 丅 下 正 正			

看	看	看	kàn: see, watch 看电视	mù 目 eye 看 看
	一 二 三 手 看			

视	视	視	shì: look at (电视: TV) 电视	jiàn 見 (见) see 视 视
	丶 ラ ネ ネ 礻 初 视 视			

Name: ________________ Date: ____________

Character	Forms	Meaning	Radical	Stroke order
做	做 做	zuò: do 做什么	rén 人(亻) person 做 做	丿 亻 亻 仁 估 估 估 做 做
网	网 網	wǎng: net 上网	jiōng 冂 borders 网 网	丨 冂 冈 网 网
就	就 就	jiù: (我就是: this is he/she speaking) 我就是	tóu 亠 cover 就 就	丶 亠 亡 亨 亨 京 京 就 就 就
位	位 位	wèi: (measure word for people, polite form) 哪位	rén 人(亻) person 位 位	亻 亻 亻 付 位
留	留 留	liú: leave; remain (留言: leave message) 留言	tián 田 land 留 留	丿 𠂉 𠂊 卯 卯 卯 留 留 留 留
言	言 言	yán: speech, words 留言	yán 言(讠) word 言 言	丶 亠 亠 言 言 言 言

时	时	時	shí: time 时候	rì 日 sun
	丨 冂 月 日 日一 时 时			时 时

候	候	候	hòu: time (时候 shíhou: time) 时候	rén 人(亻) person
	亻 亻 亻 亻 亻 亻 亻 俟 候			候 候

晚	晚	晚	wǎn: night 晚上	rì 日 sun
	日 日 日 日 日 晚 晚			晚 晚

要	要	要	yào: want, desire 要不要	yà 西(覀) cover
	一 丅 丙 襾 襾 西 覀 要 要			要 要

给	给	給	gěi: give; for, to 给我	mì 糸(纟) silk
	纟 纟 纟 纟 纟 纟 纟 给 给			给 给

Name: ______________ Date: ______________

Lesson 10 I Get Up at 7:30 Every Day

Character			Meaning	Radical
活	活	活	huó: live (生活: life) 生活	shuǐ 水(氵) water 活 活
Stroke order: 氵 氵 氵 汗 活				
期	期	期	qī: a period of time (学期: semester) 学期	ròu 肉(月) meat 期 期
Stroke order: 一 十 卄 廾 甘 甘 其 其 期				
门	门	門	mén: (M.W.) 五门课	mén 門(门) door 门 门
Stroke order: 丶 门 门				
每	每	每	měi: every, each 每天	mǔ 母 mother 每 每
Stroke order: 丿 𠂉 𠂉 乍 每 每 每				
床	床	床	chuáng: bed 起床	yǎn 广 shelter 床 床
Stroke order: 丶 亠 广 广 庄 床 床				

Character			Meaning	Radical			
睡	睡	睡	shuì: (V.) sleep 睡觉	mù 目 eye			
				睡	睡		
目	目	目	目	目	目	目	睡	睡

Character			Meaning	Radical
觉	觉	覺	jiào: (N.) sleep 睡觉	jiàn 見 (见) see
				觉 觉

Stroke order: 、 丷 ⺍ 𰀁 ⺍ 学 学 觉 觉

Character			Meaning	Radical
半	半	半	bàn: half 十二点半	zhǔ 、 segmentation symbol
				半 半

Stroke order: 、 丷 䒑 兰 半

Character			Meaning	Radical
才	才	才	cái: (used before a verb to indicate that sth. is rather late) 我十二点半才睡觉。	yī 一 one
				才 才

Stroke order: 一 十 才

Character			Meaning	Radical
刻	刻	刻	kè: a quarter (of an hour) 九点一刻	dāo 刀 (刂) knife
				刻 刻

Stroke order: 、 亠 亠 亥 亥 亥 亥 刻

Character			Meaning	Radical
分	分	分	fēn: minute 十点二十分	dāo 刀 (刂) knife
				分 分

Stroke order: 丿 八 分 分

Name: ____________ Date: ____________

然	然	然	rán: (然后 : then, afterwards) 然后	huǒ 火 (灬) fire
丿 ㇇ 夕 夕 夕一 夕𠂇 夕大 夕犬 然				

图	图	圖	tú: picture (图书馆: library) 图书馆	wéi 囗 enclosure
丨 冂 冂 冈 冈 冈 图 图				

馆	馆	館	guǎn: house, hall 图书馆	shí 食 (饣) food
丿 𠂉 饣 饣 饣 饣 饣 饣 馆 馆 馆				

午	午	午	wǔ: noon 下午	piě 丿 left slanted stroke
丿 𠂉 仁 午				

喜	喜	喜	xǐ: happy; like 喜欢	kǒu 口 mouth
一 十 士 吉 吉 吉 吉 喜				

欢	欢	歡	huān: joyfully (喜欢: like) 喜欢	qiàn 欠 owe
㇇ 又 又 欢 欢 欢				

球	球	球	qiú: ball 打球	yù 玉 (王) jade 球 球
	一 二 Ŧ 王 王一 玎 玎 玗 球 球 球			

写	写	寫	xiě: write 写信	mì 冖 cover 写 写
	丶 冖 冖 写 写			

信	信	信	xìn: letter 写信	rén 人 (亻) person 信 信
	亻 信			

子	子	子	zì: (电子: electron) 电子	zǐ 子 child 子 子
	乛 了 子			

邮	邮	郵	yóu: mail 邮件	yì 邑 (阝) city 邮 邮
	丨 冂 冃 由 由 由阝 邮			

件	件	件	jiàn: letter (邮件: mail) 邮件	rén 人 (亻) person 件 件
	丿 亻 亻' 亻仁 件 件			

Name: ____________ Date: ____________

地	地	地	dì: land 地址	tǔ 土 earth
	一 十 土 地			地 地

址	址	址	zhǐ: location 地址	tǔ 土 earth
	土 圵 圵 址 址			址 址

祝	祝	祝	zhù: wish	shì 示 (礻) reveal
	礻 祀 祝 祝			祝 祝

年	年	年	nián: year 二〇〇三年	piě 丿 left slanted stroke
	丿 𠂉 𠂉 乍 乍 年			年 年

月	月	月	yuè: month 十一月	ròu 肉 (月) meat
	丿 刀 月 月			月 月

日	日	日	rì: day 二十日	rì 日 sun
	丨 冂 日 日			日 日

Name: ______________ Date: ______________

Lesson 11 Do You Want Black Tea or Green Tea?

红	红	紅	hóng: red 红茶	mì 糸 (纟) silk

茶	茶	茶	chá: tea 喝茶	cǎo 艸 (艹) grass

还	还	還	hái: (还是: or) 还是	chuò 辵 (辶) motion

绿	绿	綠	lǜ: green 绿茶	mì 糸 (纟) silk

服	服	服	fú: serve 服务员	ròu 肉 (月) meat

务 務
wù: be engaged in
服务员
lì 力
strength
员 員
yuán: person
服务员
kǒu 口
mouth
坐 坐
zuò: sit
请坐
tǔ 土
earth
先 先
xiān:
(先生: sir, Mr.)
先生
ér 儿
walking man
喝 喝
hē: drink
喝茶
kǒu 口
mouth
杯 杯
bēi: cup
一杯红茶
mù 木
wood

Name: ____________ Date: ____________

冰	冰	冰	bīng: ice 冰红茶	bīng 冫 ice
乐	乐	樂	lè: happy (可乐: Coke) 可乐	piě 丿 left slanted stroke
瓶	瓶	瓶	píng: bottle 一瓶	wǎ 瓦 tile
啤	啤	啤	pí: (啤酒: beer) 啤酒	kǒu 口 mouth
酒	酒	酒	jiǔ: liquor, wine, alcoholic drink 啤酒	shuǐ 水(氵) water
面	面	麵	miàn: noodle 炒面	yī 一 one

Character	Simplified	Traditional	Meaning	Example	Radical
饺	饺	餃	jiǎo: dumpling	饺子	shí 食 (饣) food
盘	盘	盤	pán: plate, dish	一盘	mǐn 皿 vessel
炒	炒	炒	chǎo: fry	炒饭	huǒ 火 (灬) fire
十	十	十	shí: ten	十个饺子	shí 十 ten
碗	碗	碗	wǎn: bowl	一碗饭	shí 石 stone
汤	汤	湯	tāng: soup	一碗汤	shuǐ 水 (氵) water

Name: ____________________ Date: ______________

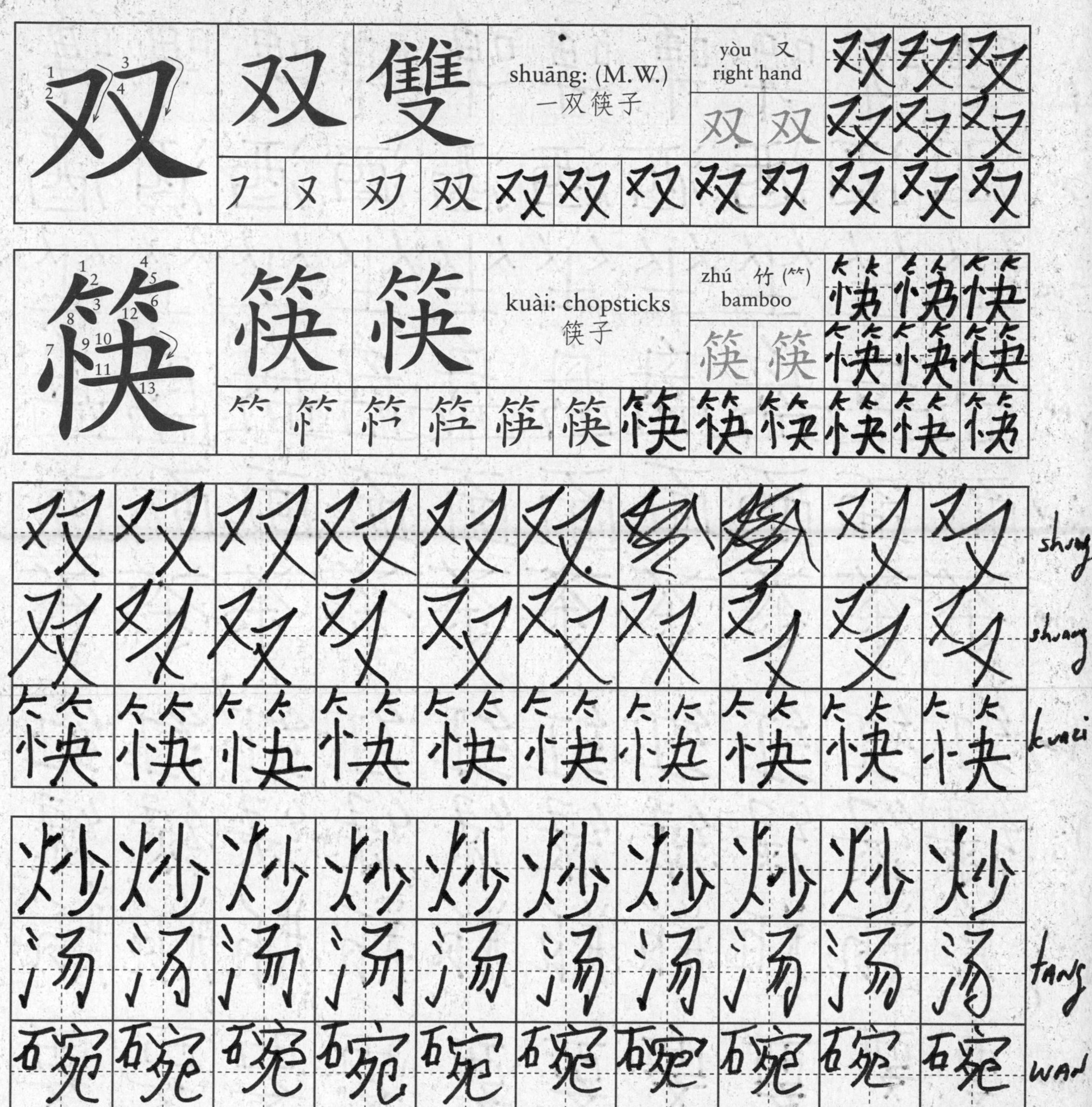
双 雙
shuāng: (M.W.)
一双筷子
yòu 又
right hand
筷 筷
kuài: chopsticks
筷子
zhú 竹 (⺮)
bamboo

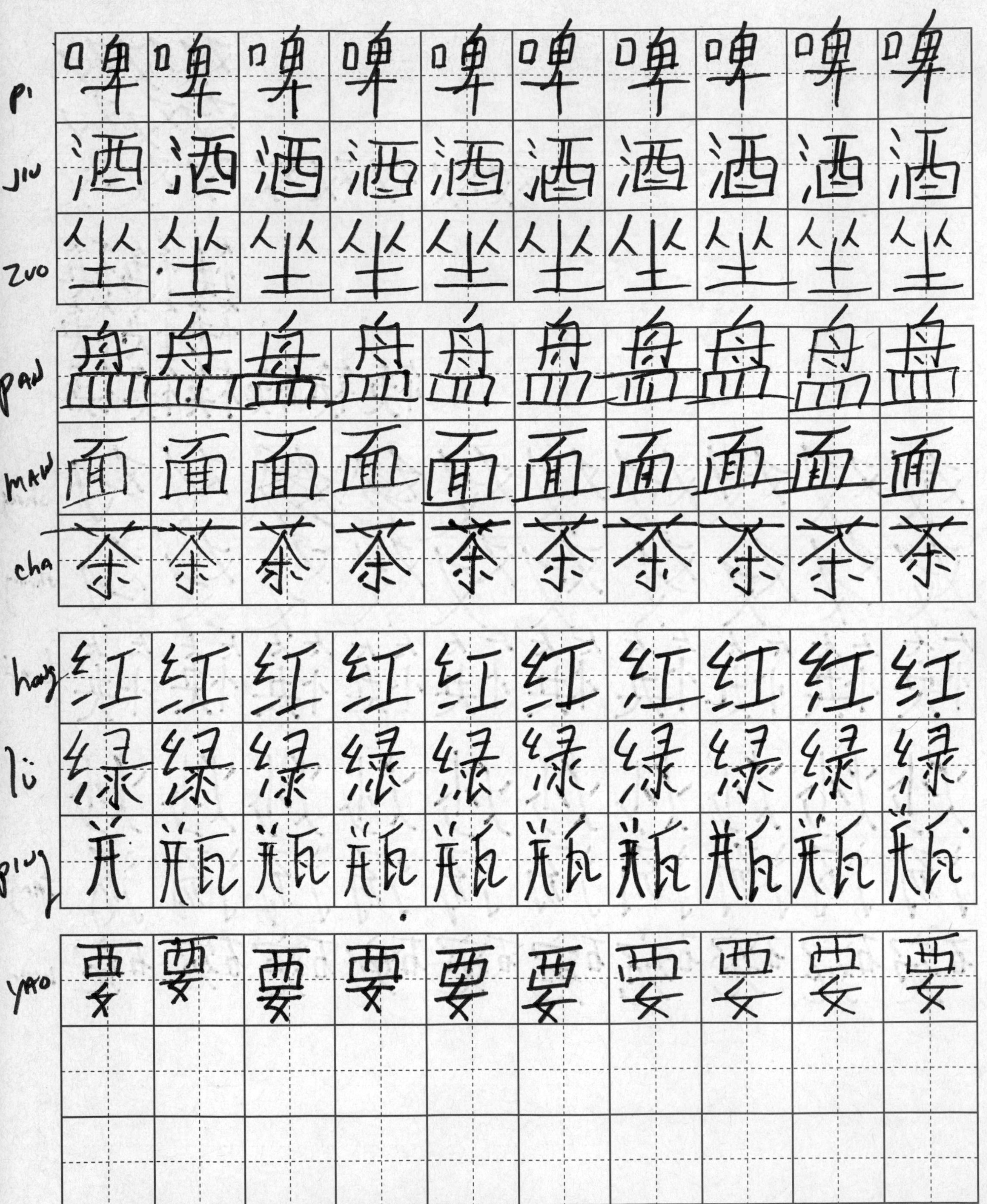

Name: ____________ Date: ____________

Lesson 12 May I Borrow Your Car?

Character	Traditional	Meaning	Radical	Tracing
借	借	jiè: borrow 借车	rén 人(亻) person	借 借
明	明	míng: bright; tomorrow 明天	rì 日 sun	明 明
用	用	yòng: use 用车	yòng 用 use	用 用
得	得	děi: have to 我得去接人。	chì 彳 step	得 得
场	場	chǎng: site, spot (机场: airport) 机场	tǔ 土 earth	场 场

Stroke order:

- 借: 亻 亻一 亻十 亻廿 亻昔 借
- 明: 日 明
- 用: 丿 冂 月 月 用
- 得: 彳 彳日 彳旦 彳旦 得 得
- 场: 一 十 土 圬 场 场

Character	Forms	Meaning	Radical	Trace
接	接 接	jiē: receive 接人	shǒu 手 (扌) hand	接 接
妹	妹 妹	mèi: younger sister 妹妹	nǚ 女 female	妹 妹
飞	飞 飛	fēi: fly 飞机	yǐ 乙 second	飞 飞
玩	玩 玩	wán: play 去玩儿	yù 玉 (王) jade	玩 玩
到	到 到	dào: arrive, reach 到我这儿来	dāo 刀 (刂) knife	到 到
排	排 排	pái: (排挡: transmission) 手排挡	shǒu 手 (扌) hand	排 排

Name: ____________ Date: ____________

挡	挡	擋	dǎng: gear (排挡: transmission) 手排挡	shǒu 手 (扌) hand
	一 十 扌 扌' 扌'' 扌'' 挡 挡 挡			

开	开	開	kāi: drive; open 开车	yī 一 one
	一 二 于 开			

应	应	應	yīng: should 应该	yǎn 广 shelter
	丶 亠 广 广 庁 应 应			

该	该	該	gāi: should 应该	yán 言 (讠) word
	丶 讠 讠' 讠亠 讠 该 该 该			

题	题	題	tí: problem; topic 问题	yè 頁 (页) head
	日 旦 早 早 昇 是 是 是 题 题 题			

白	白	白	bái: white 白色	bái 白 white
	丿 ′ 白 白 白			

Character	Simplified	Traditional	Meaning	Radical
色	色	色	sè: color 白色	dāo 刀 (刂) knife
停	停	停	tíng: stop; park 停车场	rén 人 (亻) person
习	习	習	xí: practice 练习	bīng 冫 ice
练	练	練	liàn: practice; train 练习	mì 糸 (纟) silk
能	能	能	néng: can; may; be able to 能进步	ròu 肉 (月) meat
进	进	進	jìn: move forward; enter 进步	chuò 辵 (辶) motion

Name: ____________ Date: ____________

步 (stroke order 1–7)	步	步	bù: step, pace 进步	zhǐ 止 stop
	丨 ⺊ 䒑 止 步 步 步			步 步

Name: ______________ Date: ______________

Lesson 13 I Want to Buy a Shirt

Character	Simplified	Traditional	Meaning	Radical
买	买	買	mǎi: buy 买一件衬衫	yǐ 乙 second
衬	衬	襯	chèn: (衬衫: shirt) 衬衫	yī 衣 (衤) clothing
衫	衫	衫	shān: (衬衫: shirt) 衬衫	yī 衣 (衤) clothing
店	店	店	diàn: shop 店员	yǎn 广 shelter
条	条	條	tiáo: (M.W.) 这条裙子	mù 木 wood

裙	裙	裙	qún: skirt 裙子	yī 衣 (衤) clothing
	衤 衤⁷ 衤⁷ 衤⁷ 衤尹 裙			裙 裙

或	或	或	huò: or 或者	gē 戈 spear
	一 𠮛 或 或 或 或			或 或

者	者	者	zhě: (或者: or) 或者	lǎo 耂 old
	一 十 土 耂 者			者 者

褲	裤	褲	kù: pants 裤子	yī 衣 (衤) clothing
	丶 ⺈ 衤 衤 衤 衤 衤 衤 衤 裤 裤 裤			裤 裤

黄	黄	黃	huáng: yellow 黄色	bā 八 eight
	一 十 廾 廾 共 共 共 黄 黄 黄 黄			黄 黄

错	错	錯	cuò: wrong: (不错: not bad) 不错	jīn 金 (钅) metal
	丿 𠂉 𠂉 𠂉 钅 钅 钅 钅 钅 错 错 错			错 错

Name: ____________ Date: ____________

比	比	比	bǐ: compare 比较	bǐ 比 compare 比 比
	一 ヒ ヒ 比			

较	较	較	jiào: compare 比较	chē 車 (车) vehicle 较 较
	一 ⺧ 车 车 车 车' 车亠 车六 较			

穿	穿	穿	chuān: wear 穿裙子	xué 穴 cave 穿 穿
	宀 穴 穴 穿 穿 穿 穿			

黑	黑	黑	hēi: black 黑色	hēi 黑 black 黑 黑
	丨 冂 冂 四 四 四 甲 里 黑			

试	试	試	shì: try 试试	yán 言 (讠) word 试 试
	丶 讠 讠 讠 讠 讠 试 试			

帮	帮	幫	bāng: help 帮我看看	jīn 巾 napkin 帮 帮
	一 二 三 丰 邦 邦 邦 帮 帮			

Character	Traditional	Meaning / Example	Radical
让	讓	ràng: let 让我看看。	yán 言(讠) word
钱	錢	qián: money 多少钱？	jīn 金(钅) metal
块	塊	kuài: (money) yuan; piece 十五块钱	tǔ 土 earth
张	張	zhāng: (M.W.) 一张票	gōng 弓 bow
影	影	yǐng: movie, picture 电影	shān 彡 fur
票	票	piào: ticket 电影票	shì 示(礻) reveal

Stroke order:

- 让: 丶 讠 讠 计 让
- 钱: ノ 𠂉 𠂉 乍 钅 钅 钅 钱 钱 钱
- 块: 一 十 土 圢 圢 坱 块
- 张: ㇇ コ 弓 弓 弓 张 张 张
- 影: 日 日 旦 昌 昙 昙 景 景 影 影
- 票: 一 丆 丙 丙 襾 西 覀 覀 票 票 票

Name: ____________ Date: ____________

Lesson 14 I Am 20 This Year

岁	岁	歲	suì: year (of age) 二十岁	xī 夕 night
	丨 山 山 屵 岁 岁			岁 岁

空	空	空	kòng: free time 你有没有空？	xué 穴 cave
	宀 ⺌ 穴 空			空 空

星	星	星	xīng: star (星期: week) 星期一	rì 日 sun
	日 星			星 星

过	过	過	guò: spend 过生日	chuò 辵(辶) motion
	一 寸 寸 寸 讨 过			过 过

为	为	為	wèi: for 为我	diǎn 丶 dot
	丶 ソ 为 为			为 为

舞 舞 舞
wǔ: dance (舞会: dancing party)
舞会
piě 丿
left slanted stroke
参 参 参
cān: join
(参加: attend)
参加
sī 厶
private
加 加 加
jiā: add
(参加: attend)
参加
lì 力
strength
定 定 定
dìng: surely
一定
mián 宀
roof
蛋 蛋 蛋
dàn: egg
蛋糕
chóng 虫
insect
糕 糕 糕
gāo: cake
蛋糕
mǐ 米
rice

Name: ________________ Date: ____________

送	送	送	sòng: give as a present 送你一个蛋糕	chuò 辵(辶) motion 送 送
	丶 丷 䒑 兰 关 关 关 送			

棒	棒	棒	bàng: good, excellent 太棒了！	mù 木 wood 棒 棒
	木 木 木 木 桂 柣 桂 棒 棒			

客	客	客	kè: guest, visitor (客气: polite; modest) 不客气！	mián 宀 roof 客 客
	宀 宀 穸 安 客			

气	气	氣	qì: air (客气: polite; modest) 不客气！	qì 气 air 气 气
	丿 𠂉 ⺈ 气			

Name: ________________ Date: ____________

Lesson 15 The Library Is in Front of the Dorm

Character	Simplified	Traditional	Meaning	Radical
前	前	前	qián: front 前边	dāo 刀 (刂) knife
边	边	邊	biān: (前边: front) 前边	chuò 辵 (辶) motion
迎	迎	迎	yíng: greet 欢迎	chuò 辵 (辶) motion
观	观	觀	guān: observe, look at 参观	jiàn 見 (见) see
里	里	裡	lǐ: inside 里边	lǐ 里 inside

Simplified	Traditional	Meaning	Example	Radical
厨	廚	chú: kitchen	厨房	hàn 厂 shelter
公	公	gōng: public	公用	bā 八 eight
旁	旁	páng: side	旁边	fāng 方 square
走	走	zǒu: walk	走路	zǒu 走 walk
厅	廳	tīng: hall	客厅	hàn 厂 shelter
面	面	miàn: opposite	对面	yī 一 one

Name: ____________________ Date: ______________

Character	Simplified	Traditional	Meaning	Radical
餐	餐	餐	cān: meal, food 餐厅	shí 食 (饣) food
洗	洗	洗	xǐ: wash 洗澡间	shuǐ 水 (氵) water
澡	澡	澡	zǎo: bath 洗澡	shuǐ 水 (氵) water
卧	卧	臥	wò: lie 卧室	chén 臣 official
桌	桌	桌	zhuō: desk, table 桌子	mù 木 wood
园	园	園	yuán: a piece of land 公园	wéi 囗 enclosure

真	真	真	zhēn: really, truly 真不错	shí 十 ten 真 真
1 2 3 4 5 6 7 8 9 10	一 十	真		

Name: ____________ Date: ____________

Lesson 16 She Plays Basketball Very Well

篮	篮	籃	lán: basket 篮球	zhú 竹 (⺮) bamboo
	⺮ 筌 筌 筌 筌 筌 筌 筌 篮 篮 篮			

俩	俩	倆	liǎ: two 你们俩	rén 人 (亻) person
	丿 亻 亻 亻 伒 俩 俩 俩 俩			

教	教	教	jiào/jiāo: teach 教练/教得很好	pū 攴 (攵) literacy
	一 十 土 耂 耂 考 孝 孝 孝 教 教			

游	游	游	yóu: swim 游泳游得很快	shuǐ 水 (氵) water
	氵 汸 汸 汸 游 游 游			

泳	泳	泳	yǒng: swim 游泳	shuǐ 水 (氵) water
	氵 氵 汀 汈 泳 泳			

Character			Meaning	Radical
非	非	非	fēi: wrong: not (非常: extraordinary, unusual) 非常	gǔn 丨 down stroke
快	快	快	kuài: fast 很快	xīn 心(忄) heart
体	体	體	tǐ: body 体育	rén 人(亻) person
育	育	育	yù: educate 体育	ròu 肉(月) meat
池	池	池	chí: pool 游泳池	shuǐ 水(氵) water
健	健	健	jiàn: strengthen; healthy 健身房	rén 人(亻) person

Name: ____________ Date: ____________

Character	Simplified	Traditional	Meaning	Radical
身	身	身	shēn: body 健身房	shēn 身 body
锻	锻	鍛	duàn: forge 锻炼	jīn 金 (钅) metal
炼	炼	煉	liàn: refine 锻炼	huǒ 火 (灬) fire
现	现	現	xiàn: now 现在	yù 玉 (王) jade
昨	昨	昨	zuó: yesterday 昨天	rì 日 sun
赛	赛	賽	sài: game, match 球赛	bèi 貝 (贝) shell

业 (stroke order 1–5)	业	業	yè: course of study (作业: homework) 作业	yè 业 board 业 业
	丨 丨丨 丨丨丶 业(stroke 4) 业			

包 (stroke order 1–5)	包	包	bāo: wrap 包饺子	bāo 勹 wrap 包 包
	丿 勹 匀 句 包			

慢 (stroke order 1–14)	慢	慢	màn: slow 很慢	xīn 心 (忄) heart 慢 慢
	忄 忄日 愠 慢(partial) 慢			

Name: ____________ Date: ____________

Lesson 17 Spring Is Coming Soon

Character			Meaning	Radical
春	春	春	chūn: spring 春天	rì 日 sun 春 春
Strokes: 一 二 三 丰 夫 春				
久	久	久	jiǔ: long 好久不见	piě 丿 left slanted stroke 久 久
Strokes: 丿 ク 久				
放	放	放	fàng: put, release, let go 放假	pū 攴 (攵) literacy 放 放
Strokes: 方 方 方 放 放				
假	假	假	jià: vacation, holiday 春假	rén 人 (亻) person 假 假
Strokes: 亻 亻 亻 亻 亻 亻 亻 亻 假 假				
夏	夏	夏	xià: summer 夏天	zhǐ 夊 from the end 夏 夏
Strokes: 一 丆 丆 丙 百 百 百 頁 夏 夏				

秋
qiū: fall, autumn
秋天
hé 禾
grain
冬
dōng: winter
冬天
bīng 冫
ice
其
qí: that, such
(其中: among which; whom)
其中
qí 其
he
最
zuì: most
最喜欢
yuē 曰
say
暖
nuǎn: warm
暖和
rì 日
sun
短
duǎn: short
很短
shǐ 矢
arrow

Name: ____________ Date: ____________

热	热	熱	rè: hot 非常热	huǒ 火 (灬) fire 热 热
	一 十 扌 扌 执 执 执 执 热 热			

华	华	華	huá: (华氏: Fahrenheit) 华氏	shí 十 ten 华 华
	丿 亻 亻 化 华 华			

氏	氏	氏	shì: (华氏: Fahrenheit) 华氏	piě 丿 left slanted stroke 氏 氏
	一 ㄏ 尸 氏			

百	百	百	bǎi: hundred 华氏一百度	bái 白 white 百 百
	一 ア 百			

度	度	度	dù: degree 华氏一百度	yǎn 广 shelter 度 度
	广 广 庐 庐 庐 庐 度			

极	极	極	jí: extreme 热极了	mù 木 wood 极 极
	一 十 才 木 杉 极 极			

刮	刮	刮	guā: blow 刮风	dāo 刀 (刂) knife
一 二 千 舌 刮 刮				刮 刮

风	风	風	fēng: wind 刮风	fēng 风 wind
丿 几 风 风				风 风

雨	雨	雨	yǔ: rain 下雨	yǔ 雨 rain
一 丆 冂 币 币 雨 雨 雨				雨 雨

冷	冷	冷	lěng: cold 非常冷	bīng 冫 ice
冫 冫 冷 冷 冷				冷 冷

雪	雪	雪	xuě: snow 下雪	yǔ 雨 rain
一 二 干 雨 雨 雨 雨 雪 雪 雪				雪 雪

Name: ____________ Date: ____________

Lesson 18 We Are Going to Take a Train Trip

Character			Meaning	Radical
火	火	火	huǒ: fire (火车: train) 火车	huǒ 火 (灬) fire
旅	旅	旅	lǚ: travel 旅行	fāng 方 square
离	离	離	lí: leave, part from, away 离学校不远	tóu 亠 cover
远	远	遠	yuǎn: far, distant 不远	chuò 辵 (辶) motion
只	只	只	zhǐ: only 只要	kǒu 口 mouth

钟	钟	鐘	zhōng: clock 分钟	jīn 金(钅) metal
	丿 ⺈ 𠂉 ⺧ 钅 钅 钔 钔 钟			钟 钟

骑	骑	騎	qí: ride 骑自行车	mǎ 馬(马) horse
	𠃍 马 马 马 马 马 骂 骑 骑 骑 骑			骑 骑

自	自	自	zì: self 自行车	zì 自 self
	丿 亻 门 白 自 自			自 自

共	共	共	gòng: common, general 公共汽车	bā 八 eight
	一 十 卄 廾 共 共			共 共

汽	汽	汽	qì: steam, vapor 汽车	shuǐ 水(氵) water
	氵 氵 汇 汽 汽			汽 汽

路	路	路	lù: road 走路	zú 足 foot
	口 早 早 𧾷 𧾷 𧾷 路 路 路			路 路

Name: ____________________ Date: ______________

近 近 近

jìn: near, close
很近

chuò 辵 (辶)
motion

汽近

丿 𠂆 斤 斤 近

西 西 西

xī: west
西部

xī 西
perch

西 西

一 丆 丙 丙 两 西

部 部 部

bù: part
西部

yì 邑 (阝)
city

部 部

丶 亠 亠 立 立 音 咅 部

景 景 景

jǐng: view, scenery
风景

rì 日
sun

景 景

日 旦 昱 昌 亭 景 景

船 船 船

chuán: boat, ship
坐船

zhōu 舟
boat

船 船

丿 丿 月 月 舟 舟 舟 舡 舡 船 船

南 南 南

nán: south
南部

shí 十
ten

南 南

一 十 𠂇 冂 冂 冇 卉 南 南

听	听	聽	tīng: listen 听说	kǒu 口 mouth 听 听
	丨 口 口 口´ 叮 听 听			

海	海	海	hǎi: sea 海边	shuǐ 水 (氵) water 海 海
	氵 氵 氵 汇 海 海 海 海			

租	租	租	zū: rent 租车	hé 禾 grain 租 租
	禾 利 和 和 租 租			

Name: ____________ Date: ____________

Lesson 19 I Caught a Cold

感	感	感	gǎn: feel, sense (感冒: cold; catch a cold) 感冒	xīn 心 (忄) heart
丿	厂	厂	后	咸 咸 咸 感

冒	冒	冒	mào: emit, give off (感冒: cold; catch a cold) 感冒	yuē 曰 say
丶	冂	冃	冃	冃 冃 冐 冒 冒

饿	饿	餓	è: hungry 我不饿。	shí 食 (饣) food
丿	𠂊	饣	饣	饣 饤 饫 饿 饿 饿

像	像	像	xiàng: be like; seem 好像	rén 人 (亻) person
亻	亻	亻	亻	傍 侉 像 像 像 像 像

舒	舒	舒	shū: loosen, relax 舒服	rén 人 (亻) person
丿	人	人	亼	午 舍 舍 舍 舒 舒

Character	Traditional	Meaning	Word	Radical	Stroke sequence
头	頭	tóu: head	头疼	zhǔ 丶 segmentation symbol	丶 ⺀ 䒑 头 头
疼	疼	téng: ache; pain	头疼	nè 疒 sick	丶 亠 广 疒 疒 疼
发	發	fā: feel; send out	发烧	yòu 又 right hand	𠃋 十 发 发 发
烧	燒	shāo: fever	发烧	huǒ 火 (灬) fire	丶 丷 少 火 灯 炷 烧 烧 烧 烧
咳	咳	ké: cough	咳嗽	kǒu 口 mouth	口 咳
嗽	嗽	sòu: (咳嗽: cough)	咳嗽	kǒu 口 mouth	口 口 口 叮 叮 呻 啤 嗽 嗽 嗽

Name: ____________ Date: ____________

Character	Simplified	Traditional	Meaning	Radical
病	病	病	bìng: be taken ill; disease 生病	nè 疒 sick
考	考	考	kǎo: give or take an exam, a test or a quiz 考试	lǎo 耂 old
复	复	復	fù: repeat (复习: review) 复习	pū 攴(攵) literacy
所	所	所	suǒ: (所以: therefore) 所以	jīn 斤 axe
医	医	醫	yī: doctor; medical science 医生	fāng 匚 square vessel
药	药	藥	yào: medicine 吃药	cǎo 艸(艹) grass

休	休	休	xiū: rest 休息	rén 人(亻) person
	亻	仁	什	付	休

息	息	息	xī: rest (休息: xiūxi) 休息	xīn 心(忄) heart
	′	自	息

准	准	準	zhǔn: (准备: prepare; plan) 准备	bīng 冫 ice
	、	冫	丫	丬	汁	汴	浐	洚	准	准

备	备	備	bèi: prepare, get ready 准备	zhǐ 夂 from the end
	丿	ク	夂	夂	各	咨	备	备

笔	笔	筆	bǐ: notes; record 笔记	zhú 竹(⺮) bamboo
	丿	𠂉	𠂉	𥫗	𥫗	⺮	笋	笁	笔	笔

记	记	記	jì: notes; record 笔记	yán 言(讠) word
	、	讠	订	订	记

Name: ______________ Date: ______________

Lesson 20 I've Brought Xiao Xie Over . . .

把	把	把	bǎ: (Prep.) 我把车开回来了。	shǒu 手 (扌) hand
	扌 扌 扣 扣 把			把 把

带	带	带	dài: bring 带来	jīn 巾 napkin
	一 十 卄 卅 卅 卅 带 带 带			带 带

啊	啊	啊	a: (Int.) 是小谢啊！	kǒu 口 mouth
	口 叮 叩 叩 啊 啊			啊 啊

搬	搬	搬	bān: move 搬出去	shǒu 手 (扌) hand
	扌 揤 搬			搬 搬

出	出	出	chū: out 搬出去	kǎn 凵 hole
	乚 凵 屮 出 出			出 出

吸	吸	吸	xī: inhale 吸烟	kǒu 口 mouth 吸 吸
	丨 ㄇ 口 口丿 吸 吸			

烟	烟	煙	yān: smoke; cigarette 吸烟	huǒ 火 (灬) fire 烟 烟
	丶 丷 火 火 火 灯 炯 炯 炯 烟			

关	关	關	guān: concern 关系	bā 八 eight 关 关
	丶 丷 丷 兰 关 关			

系	系	係	xì: relate to 关系	mì 糸 silk 系 系
	一 𠂉 玄 玄 系 系 系			

但	但	但	dàn: but 但是	rén 人 (亻) person 但 但
	亻 伯 但			

女	女	女	nǚ: female 女朋友	nǚ 女 female 女 女
	𡿨 女 女			

Name: ____________ Date: ____________

必	必	必	bì: must, have to 必须	xīn 心 (忄) heart 必 必
	丶 心 心 必 必			

须	须	須	xū: must, have to 必须	yè 頁 (页) head 须 须
	丿 彡 彡 彡 彡 彡 须 须 须			

第	第	第	dì: (prefix for ordinal numbers) 第一天	zhú 竹 (⺮) bamboo 第 第
	⺮ 笃 笃 笃 第 第			

付	付	付	fù: pay 付房租	rén 人 (亻) person 付 付
	亻 仁 付 付			

楼	楼	樓	lóu: floor 楼上	mù 木 wood 楼 楼
	一 十 才 木 木 术 朩 栏 柈 楼 楼			

马	马	馬	mǎ: horse (马上: at once) 马上	mǎ 馬 (马) horse 马 马
	㇇ 马 马			

Name: ____________ Date: ____________

Lesson 21 What Will You Do During the Summer Vacation?

Character	Forms	Meaning	Radical	Stroke order
暑	暑 暑	shǔ: heat, hot weather 暑假	rì 日 sun	暑
毕	毕 畢	bì: finish, accomplish 毕业	bǐ 比 compare	比 毕
决	决 决	jué: decide 决定	bīng 冫 ice	冫 决
申	申 申	shēn: state, express 申请	tián 田 land	申
研	研 研	yán: study 研究	shí 石 stone	石 研

究	究	究	jiū: study carefully; investigate 研究	xué 穴 cave	究 究
	丶 丶 宀 宀 穴 究 究				
院	院	院	yuàn: institute 研究院	fù 阜 (阝) hill	院 院
	阝 阝 阝 阝 阝 院				
找	找	找	zhǎo: look for 找工作	shǒu 手 (扌) hand	找 找
	扌 扌 扌 找 找				
司	司	司	sī: department 公司	kǒu 口 mouth	司 司
	丁 ㇆ 司				
实	实	實	shí: solid; true (实习: intern) 实习	mián 宀 roof	实 实
	丶 丶 宀 宀 宀 宀 实 实				
脑	脑	腦	nǎo: brain 电脑	ròu 肉 (月) moon	脑 脑
	丿 月 月 月 月 月 月 月 脑 脑				

Name: ______________ Date: ______________

班	班	班	bān: class 暑期班	yù 玉 (王) jade 班 班
	一 二 干 王 王 玎 玒 玟 班 班			

意	意	意	yì: meaning 意思	xīn 心 (忄) heart 意 意
	丶 亠 亠 立 立 音 意			

思	思	思	sī: think, consider (意思: yìsi) 有意思	xīn 心 (忄) heart 思 思
	丨 冂 日 田 田 思			

愉	愉	愉	yú: happy 愉快	xīn 心 (忄) heart 愉 愉
	忄 忄 忙 怜 愉 愉 愉			

平	平	平	píng: calm, peaceful 平安	yī 一 one 平 平
	一 丆 丆 立 平			

安	安	安	ān: safe 平安	mián 宀 roof 安 安
	宀 它 安 安			

运 運

yùn: luck
好运

chuò 辵(辶) motion

运 运

一 二 云 云 运 运 运

Name: ____________ Date: ____________

Lesson 22 I Have Arrived in Shanghai

因	因	因	yīn: because 因为	wéi 囗 enclosure 因 因
	冂 冂 冃 冈 因 因			
已	已	已	yǐ: already (已经: already) 已经	jǐ 己 self 已 已
	㇆ コ 已			
经	经	經	jīng: pass (已经: already) 已经	mì 糸 (纟) silk 经 经
	𠃋 纟 纟 纟 经 经 经 经			
丽	丽	麗	lì: beautiful 美丽	yī 一 one 丽 丽
	一 丅 丆 丙 丽 丽 丽			
城	城	城	chéng: city 城市	tǔ 土 earth 城 城
	土 圵 圹 坊 城 城 城			

市	市	市	shì: city 城市	jīn 巾 napkin
	丶 亠 广 市 市			市 市

处	处	處	chù: place 到处	zhǐ 夂 from the end
	丿 ㄅ 夂 処 处			处 处

新	新	新	xīn: new 新的大楼	jīn 斤 ax
	丶 亠 亠 立 立 立 辛 辛 亲 新 新 新			新 新

些	些	些	xiē: some 一些	bǐ 匕 dagger
	丨 卜 卜 止 止 此 此 些			些 些

方	方	方	fāng: direction; side 地方	fāng 方 place
	丶 亠 方 方			方 方

动	动	動	dòng: move 活动	lì 力 strength
	一 二 云 云 动 动			动 动

Name: ____________ Date: ____________

Character	Simplified	Traditional	Meaning	Radical
如	如	如	rú: be like; as if 比如	nǚ 女 female
京	京	京	jīng: Beijing; the capital of a country 京剧	tóu 亠 cover
剧	剧	劇	jù: opera, play, drama 京剧	dāo 刀(刂) knife
东	东	東	dōng: east (东西: thing) 东西	yī 一 one
笼	笼	籠	lóng: cage; steamer 小笼包	zhú 竹(⺮) bamboo
尝	尝	嚐	cháng: taste 尝尝	xiǎo 小 little

始	始	始	shǐ: beginning 开始	nǚ 女 female
	女	女𠃋	女厶	始

高	高	高	gāo: high 高兴	tóu 亠 cover
	丶	亠	古	亠冂	亠冋	高

兴	兴	興	xìng: pleasure 高兴	bā 八 eight
	丶	丷	䒑	业	业丿	兴

收	收	收	shōu: receive 收到	pū 攴(攵) literacy
	乚	丩	丩丿	丩𠂉	收	收

心	心	心	xīn: heart 开心	xīn 心(忄) heart
	丿	心	心	心

板	板	闆	bǎn: board, plate (老板: boss) 老板	mù 木 wood
	一	十	才	木	木丿	木厂	板	板

Name: ________________ Date: ____________

保	保	保	bǎo: protect; maintain 保重	rén 人 (亻) person
	亻	伊	俘	保

重	重	重	zhòng: heavy 保重	lǐ 里 hamlet

写字簿生词索引 CHARACTER BOOK INDEX (BY NUMBER OF STROKES)

Each entry lists simplified character, traditional character, Pinyin, English meaning, and lesson number.

9

13

14

15

16

写字簿生词索引 CHARACTER BOOK INDEX (BY LESSON NUMBER)

Each entry lists simplified character, traditional character, Pinyin, and English meaning.

Lesson 1

你		nǐ	you
好		hǎo	good
是		shì	is, are
学	學	xué	study
生		shēng	student
吗	嗎	ma	Part.
我		wǒ	I, me
呢		ne	Part.
也		yě	also, too
他		tā	he, him
不		bù	not
老		lǎo	old
师	師	shī	teacher

Lesson 2

您		nín	(polite) you
贵	貴	guì	noble, honored
姓		xìng	family name
请	請	qǐng	please
问	問	wèn	ask
的		de	Part.
英		yīng	英文: English
文		wén	language, writing
名		míng	name
字		zì	character, word
中		zhōng	middle
叫		jiào	call
什		shén	什么: what
么	麼	me	什么: what
她		tā	she, her
谁	誰	shéi	who, whom
同		tóng	same, similar

Lesson 3

哪		nǎ	which
国	國	guó	country
人		rén	person
很		hěn	very
对	對	duì	correct
了		le	Part.
法		fǎ	法国: France
美		měi	beautiful
说	說	shuō	speak
会	會	huì	be able to
一		yī	one
点	點	diǎn	dot
儿	兒	ér	(retroflex ending)
和		hé	and

Lesson 4

那		nà	that
书	書	shū	book
这	這	zhè	this
本		běn	M.W.
工		gōng	work
程		chéng	工程: engineering
难	難	nán	difficult
太		tài	too
可		kě	but
功		gōng	功课: homework
课	課	kè	class
多		duō	many, much
们	們	men	(suffix)
少		shǎo	few, little

Lesson 5

朋		péng	friend
友		yǒu	friend
来	來	lái	come
介		jiè	介绍: introduce
绍	紹	shào	介绍: introduce
下		xià	down; get off
室		shì	room
有		yǒu	have
几	幾	jǐ	how many
两	兩	liǎng	two
个	個	gè	M.W.
都		dōu	all; both
常		cháng	often
跟		gēn	with

Lesson 6

家		jiā	home
大		dà	big
从	從	cóng	from
在		zài	at, in
四		sì	four
爸		bà	dad
妈	媽	mā	mom
姐		jiě	older sister
作		zuò	工作: work
男		nán	male
没	沒	méi	don't have
辆	輛	liàng	M.W. for vehicles
车	車	chē	car
只	隻	zhī	M.W.
狗		gǒu	dog
爱	愛	ài	love

Lesson 7

住		zhù	live
宿		sù	stay overnight
舍		shè	house
号	號	hào	number
房		fáng	house
间	間	jiān	room
电	電	diàn	electricity
话	話	huà	word
小		xiǎo	small
码	碼	mǎ	number
二		èr	two
三		sān	three
五		wǔ	five
六		liù	six
七		qī	seven
八		bā	eight
九		jiǔ	nine
手		shǒu	hand
机	機	jī	machine
校		xiào	school
外		wài	outside

Lesson 8

认	認	rèn	know, recognize
识	識	shí	know, recognize
去		qù	go
上		shàng	get on, attend
以		yǐ	以后: after, later
后	後	hòu	behind
事		shì	matter, thing
想		xiǎng	want, think
回		huí	return
起		qǐ	一起: together
吃		chī	eat
饭	飯	fàn	rice, meal
菜		cài	dish
今		jīn	today
天		tiān	day
次		cì	order, sequence
怎		zěn	how
样	樣	yàng	appearance
行		xíng	okay
再		zài	again
见	見	jiàn	see

Lesson 9

打		dǎ	hit, play, make
喂		wèi/wéi	hello, hey
等		děng	wait

知		zhī	know
道		dào	road, walk
谢	謝	xiè	thanks
吧		ba	Part.
忙		máng	busy
正		zhèng	in process of
看		kàn	see, watch
视	視	shì	look
做		zuò	do
网	網	wǎng	net
就		jiù	Adv.
位		wèi	M.W.
留		liú	leave, remain
言		yán	speech, words
时	時	shí	time
候		hòu	time
晚		wǎn	night, late
要		yào	want
给	給	gěi	give; for, to

Lesson 10

活		huó	live
期		qī	a period of time
门	門	mén	M.W.
每		měi	every, each
床		chuáng	bed
睡		shuì	sleep
觉	覺	jiào	sleep
半		bàn	half
才		cái	Adv.
刻		kè	a quarter
分		fēn	minute
然		rán	然后: then
图	圖	tú	picture
馆	館	guǎn	house, hall
午		wǔ	noon
喜		xǐ	happy; like
欢	歡	huān	joyfully
球		qiú	ball
写	寫	xiě	write
信		xìn	letter
子		zǐ	(suffix)
邮	郵	yóu	mail
件		jiàn	letter
地		dì	land
址		zhǐ	location
祝		zhù	wish
年		nián	year
月		yuè	month
日		rì	day

Lesson 11

红	紅	hóng	red
茶		chá	tea
还	還	hái	还是: or
绿	綠	lǜ	green
服		fú	serve
务	務	wù	be engaged in
员	員	yuán	person
坐		zuò	sit
先		xiān	先生: sir, Mr.
喝		hē	drink
杯		bēi	cup
冰		bīng	ice
乐	樂	lè	happy
瓶		píng	bottle
啤		pí	beer
酒		jiǔ	liquor
面	麵	miàn	noodle
饺	餃	jiǎo	dumpling
盘	盤	pán	plate
炒		chǎo	fry
十		shí	ten
碗		wǎn	bowl
汤	湯	tāng	soup
双	雙	shuāng	pair
筷		kuài	chopsticks

Lesson 12

借		jiè	borrow
明		míng	tomorrow
用		yòng	use
得		děi	have to
场	場	chǎng	site
接		jiē	receive

妹		mèi	younger sister
飞	飛	fēi	fly
玩		wán	play
到		dào	arrive
排		pái	line
挡	擋	dǎng	gear
开	開	kāi	drive
应	應	yīng	should
该	該	gāi	should
题	題	tí	problem, topic
白		bái	white
色		sè	color
停		tíng	stop, park
习	習	xí	practice
练	練	liàn	practice
能		néng	can, may
进	進	jìn	move forward
步		bù	step

Lesson 13

买	買	mǎi	buy
衬	襯	chèn	衬衫: shirt
衫		shān	shirt, clothes
店		diàn	shop
条	條	tiáo	M.W.
裙		qún	skirt
或		huò	or
者		zhě	或者: or
裤	褲	kù	pants
黄	黃	huáng	yellow
错	錯	cuò	wrong
比		bǐ	compare
较	較	jiào	compare
穿		chuān	wear
黑		hēi	black
试	試	shì	try
帮	幫	bāng	help
让	讓	ràng	let
钱	錢	qián	money
块	塊	kuài	dollar
张	張	zhāng	M.W.
影		yǐng	shadow, movie
票		piào	ticket

Lesson 14

岁	歲	suì	year (of age)
空		kòng	free time
星		xīng	star
过	過	guò	spend
为	為	wèi	for
舞		wǔ	dance
参	參	cān	join
加		jiā	add
定		dìng	surely
蛋		dàn	egg
糕		gāo	cake
送		sòng	give as a present
棒		bàng	good, excellent
客		kè	guest
气	氣	qì	air

Lesson 15

前		qián	front
边	邊	biān	side
迎		yíng	greet
观	觀	guān	observe
里	裡	lǐ	inside
厨	廚	chú	kitchen
公		gōng	public
旁		páng	side
走		zǒu	walk
厅	廳	tīng	hall
面		miàn	surface
餐		cān	meal, food
洗		xǐ	wash
澡		zǎo	bath
卧	臥	wò	lie
桌		zhuō	table
园	園	yuán	a piece of land
真		zhēn	really

Lesson 16

篮	籃	lán	basket
俩	倆	liǎ	two
教		jiào/jiāo	teach

游		yóu	swim
泳		yǒng	swim
非		fēi	wrong, not
快		kuài	fast
体	體	tǐ	body
育		yù	educate
池		chí	pool
健		jiàn	healthy
身		shēn	body
锻	鍛	duàn	forge
炼	煉	liàn	refine
现	現	xiàn	now
昨		zuó	yesterday
赛	賽	sài	game, match
业	業	yè	course of study
包		bāo	wrap
慢		màn	slow

Lesson 17

春		chūn	spring
久		jiǔ	long
放		fàng	put, release
假		jià	vacation
夏		xià	summer
秋		qiū	fall, autumn
冬		dōng	winter
其		qí	that, such
最		zuì	most
暖		nuǎn	warm
短		duǎn	short
热	熱	rè	hot
华	華	huá	华氏: Fahrenheit
氏		shì	华氏: Fahrenheit
百		bǎi	hundred
度		dù	degree
极	極	jí	extreme
刮		guā	blow
风	風	fēng	wind
雨		yǔ	rain
冷		lěng	cold
雪		xuě	snow

Lesson 18

火		huǒ	fire
旅		lǚ	travel
离	離	lí	leave, part from
远	遠	yuǎn	far
只		zhǐ	only
钟	鐘	zhōng	clock
骑	騎	qí	ride
自		zì	self
共		gòng	common
汽		qì	steam
路		lù	road
近		jìn	close
西		xī	west
部		bù	part
景		jǐng	view, scenery
船		chuán	boat, ship
南		nán	south
听	聽	tīng	listen
海		hǎi	sea
租		zū	rent

Lesson 19

感		gǎn	feel, sense
冒		mào	emit, give off
饿	餓	è	hungry
像		xiàng	be like; seem
舒		shū	loosen, relax
头	頭	tóu	head
疼		téng	ache, pain
发	發	fā	feel, send out
烧	燒	shāo	fever
咳		ké	cough
嗽		sòu	cough
病		bìng	sick
考		kǎo	give or take a test
复	復	fù	repeat
所		suǒ	所以: therefore
医	醫	yī	medical science
药	藥	yào	medicine
休		xiū	休息: rest

息		xī	rest
准	準	zhǔn	prepare
备	備	bèi	prepare
笔	筆	bǐ	pen
记	記	jì	notes

Lesson 20

把		bǎ	Prep.
带	帶	dài	bring
啊		a	Int.
搬		bān	move
出		chū	out
吸		xī	inhale
烟	煙	yān	smoke
关	關	guān	concern
系	係	xì	relate to
但		dàn	but
女		nǚ	female
必		bì	must
须	須	xū	must
第		dì	(prefix)
付		fù	pay
楼	樓	lóu	floor
马	馬	mǎ	horse

Lesson 21

暑		shǔ	heat, hot
毕	畢	bì	finish
决	決	jué	decide
申		shēn	express
研		yán	study
究		jiū	study
院		yuàn	institute
找		zhǎo	look for
司		sī	department
实	實	shí	solid
脑	腦	nǎo	brain
班		bān	class
意		yì	meaning
思		sī	think
愉		yú	happy
平		píng	calm, peaceful
安		ān	safe
运	運	yùn	luck

Lesson 22

因		yīn	because
已		yǐ	already
经	經	jīng	pass
丽	麗	lì	beautiful
城		chéng	city
市		shì	city
处	處	chù	place
新		xīn	new
些		xiē	some
方		fāng	side, direction
动	動	dòng	move
如		rú	be like
京		jīng	capital
剧	劇	jù	opera, drama
东	東	dōng	east
笼	籠	lóng	cage, steamer
尝	嚐	cháng	taste
始		shǐ	beginning
高		gāo	high
兴	興	xìng	pleasure
收		shōu	receive
心		xīn	heart
板	闆	bǎn	老板: boss
保		bǎo	protect, maintain
重		zhòng	heavy

写字簿生词索引 CHARACTER BOOK INDEX (ALPHABETICAL BY PINYIN)

Each entry lists simplified character, traditional character, Pinyin, English meaning, and lesson number.

N

P

Q

R

S

T

W

X

Y

Z

Name: ____________ Date: ____________

Name: ________________ Date: ____________

Name: ____________________ Date: ______________

Name: ______________ Date: __________

Name: ________________ Date: ____________

Name: ____________ Date: ____________

Name: ____________________ Date: ______________

Name: ____________________ Date: ______________

Name: ____________________ Date: ______________

Name: ________________ Date: ____________